Microwave Magic
Veal and Lamb

Grolier Limited
TORONTO

Contributors to this series:

Recipes and Technical Assistance:
École de cuisine Bachand-Bissonnette
Cooking consultants:
Denis Bissonette
Michèle Émond
Dietician:
Christiane Barbeau
Photos:
Laramée Morel Communications
Audio-Visuelles
Design:
Claudette Taillefer
Assistants:
Julie Deslauriers
Philippe O'Connor
Joan Pothier
Accessories:
Andrée Cournoyer
Writing:
Communications La Griffe Inc.
Text Consultants:
Cap et bc inc.
Advisors:
Roger Aubin
Joseph R. De Varennes
Gaston Lavoie
Kenneth H. Pearson

Assembly:
Carole Garon
Vital Lapalme
Jean-Pierre Larose
Carl Simmons
Gus Soriano
Marc Vallières
Production Managers:
Gilles Chamberland
Ernest Homewood
Production Assistants:
Martine Gingras
Catherine Gordon
Kathy Kishimoto
Peter Thomlison
Art Director:
Bernard Lamy
Editors:
Laurielle Ilacqua
Susan Marshall
Margaret Oliver
Robin Rivers
Lois Rock
Jocelyn Smyth
Donna Thomson
Dolores Williams
Development:
Le Groupe Polygone Éditeurs Inc.

We wish to thank the following firms, PIER I IMPORTS and LE CACHE POT, for their contribution to the illustration of this set.

The series editors have taken every care to ensure that the information given is accurate. However, no cookbook can guarantee the user successful results. The editors cannot accept any responsibility for the results obtained by following the recipes and recommendations given.

Canadian Cataloguing in Publication Data

Main entry under title:

Veal and lamb

(Microwave magic ; 10)
Translation of: Veau et agneau.
Includes index.
ISBN 0-7172-2431-7

1. Cookery (Veal).   2. Cookery (Lamb and mutton).
3. Microwave cookery.   I. Series: Microwave magic (Toronto, Ont.) ; 10.

TX832.V4213 1988   641.6'62   C88-094209-6

Contents

Microwave Magic is a multi-volume set, with each volume devoted to a particular type of cooking. So, if you are looking for a chicken recipe, you simply go to one of the two volumes that deal with poultry. Each volume has its own index, and the final volume contains a general index to the complete set.

Microwave Magic puts over twelve hundred recipes at your fingertips. You will find it as useful as the microwave oven itself. Enjoy!

Note from the Editor

How to Use this Book
The books in this set have been designed to make your job as easy as possible. As a result, most of the recipes are set out in a standard way.

We suggest that you begin by consulting the information chart for the recipe you have chosen. You will find there all the information you need to decide if you are able to make it: preparation time, cost per serving, level of difficulty, number of calories per serving and other relevant details. Thus, if you have only 30 minutes in which to prepare the evening meal, you will quickly be able to tell which recipe is possible and suits your schedule.

The list of ingredients is always clearly separated from the main text. When space allows, the ingredients are shown together in a photograph so that you can make sure you have them all without rereading the list—

another way of saving your valuable time. In addition, for the more complex recipes we have supplied photographs of the key stages involved either in preparation or serving.

All the dishes in this book have been cooked in a 700 watt microwave oven. If your oven has a different wattage, consult the conversion chart that appears on the following page for cooking times in different types of oven. We would like to emphasize that the cooking times given in the book are a minimum. If a dish does not seem to be cooked enough, you may return it to the oven for a few more minutes. Also, the cooking time can vary according to your ingredients: their water and fat content, thickness, shape and even where they come from. We have therefore left a blank space on each recipe page in which you can note

the cooking time that suits you best. This will enable you to add a personal touch to the recipes that we suggest and to reproduce your best results every time.

Although we have put all the technical information together at the front of this book, we have inserted a number of boxed entries called **MICROTIPS** throughout to explain particular techniques. They are brief and simple, and will help you obtain successful results in your cooking.

With the very first recipe you try, you will discover just how simple microwave cooking can be and how often it depends on techniques you already use for cooking with a conventional oven. If cooking is a pleasure for you, as it is for us, it will be all the more so with a microwave oven. Now let's get on with the food.

The Editor

Key to the Symbols
For ease of reference, the following symbols have been used on the recipe information charts.

The pencil symbol is a reminder to write your cooking time in the space provided.

Level of Difficulty

🍴 Easy

🍴🍴 Moderate

🍴🍴🍴 Complex

Cost per Serving

$ Inexpensive

$ $ Moderate

$ $ $ Expensive

Power Levels

All the recipes in this book have been tested in a 700 watt oven. As there are many microwave ovens on the market with different power levels, and as the names of these levels vary from one manufacturer to another, we have decided to give power levels as a percentage. To adapt the power levels given here, consult the chart opposite and the instruction manual for your oven.

Generally speaking, if you have a 500 watt or 600 watt oven you should increase cooking times by about 30% over those given, depending on the actual length of time required. The shorter the original cooking time, the greater the percentage by which it must be lengthened. The 30% figure is only an average. Consult the chart for detailed information on this topic.

Power Levels

HIGH: 100% - 90%	Vegetables (except boiled potatoes and carrots) Soup Sauce Fruits Browning ground beef Browning dish Popcorn
MEDIUM HIGH: 80% - 70%	Rapid defrosting of precooked dishes Muffins Some cakes Hot dogs
MEDIUM: 60% - 50%	Cooking tender meat Cakes Fish Seafood Eggs Reheating Boiled potatoes and carrots
MEDIUM LOW: 40%	Cooking less tender meat Simmering Melting chocolate
DEFROST: 30% **LOW: 30% - 20%**	Defrosting Simmering Cooking less tender meat
WARM: 10%	Keeping food warm Allowing yeast dough to rise

Cooking Time Conversion Chart

700 watts	600 watts*
5 s	11 s
15 s	20 s
30 s	40 s
45 s	1 min
1 min	1 min 20 s
2 min	2 min 40 s
3 min	4 min
4 min	5 min 20 s
5 min	6 min 40 s
6 min	8 min
7 min	9 min 20 s
8 min	10 min 40 s
9 min	12 min
10 min	13 min 30 s
20 min	26 min 40 s
30 min	40 min
40 min	53 min 40 s
50 min	66 min 40 s
1 h	1 h 20 min

* There is very little difference in cooking times between 500 watt ovens and 600 watt ovens.

Veal and Lamb: Bringing Springtime to Your Table

Although veal and lamb are two very different types of meat, they are closely linked in our culture; we associate them with springtime and the celebrations and feast days that take place at that time of year.

For thousands of years, in fact, veal and lamb have been part of springtime festivities —the reason being that when breeding was left to nature, calving and lambing only took place in that season. And although modern methods have made it possible for us to control breeding and animals are now born throughout the year, we still eat veal and lamb mainly in the spring.

Calf breeding, as we know it, was obviously initiated when people began to raise cattle. It seems that the first efforts to tame the wild ox date back about 8,000 years and can be traced back to Macedonia and Turkey. Since then, hundreds of new breeds and crossbreeds have sprung up all over the world.

As for sheep raising, its origins seem to go back even farther, because the nomadic peoples of central Asia tamed the wild sheep about 10,000 years ago. Later, raising sheep became more systematic in the Middle East and spread to China, India, North Africa and Europe, where sheep were prized above all for their wool. It wasn't until the eighteenth century that sheep began to be raised for their meat. New techniques came into play through experiments in crossbreeding, that succeeded in developing new breeds and plumper animals with more tender meat. Modern breeding methods owe a lot to discoveries made in the last century.

Veal and lamb are far from equal as far as consumption goes—we eat far more veal than lamb in this country. Beef accounts for a major part of our market and our pastures are rich enough to feed all our cattle until they reach adulthood. Veal is more a by-product of the dairy industry; the young calves that aren't necessary to renew the herds are sent early on to the slaughterhouse. In our culture, then, veal owes its popularity to the popularity of beef.

Compared with beef and veal, we eat an incredibly small amount of lamb—50 times less! This may be because unsophisticated methods are still used in sheep breeding Consequently, its availability on our market has never been regular and the meat is then more expensive than other meats. As well, frozen lamb, mainly from New Zealand and Australia, is far easier to find in our stores than fresh lamb. So we are caught in a vicious circle; we do not appreciate lamb because we produce too little of it, but we produce too little because it is less in demand. It is members of ethnic communities—from the Mediterranean, especially—who eat the most lamb in our country since it is used as a base in many of their traditional dishes. Perhaps it is time for us to follow their example.

Cuts of Veal

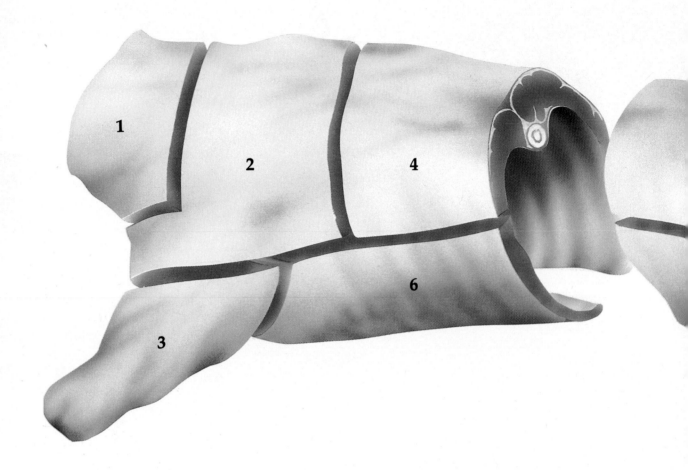

1. The Neck. The neck is usually cut into cubes or chunks for stewing.

2. The Shoulder. Situated above the foreshank, this part is mainly cut into blade steaks, shoulder chops and shoulder roasts. The latter are usually boned and rolled, and may be dry roasted or braised. The shoulder can also be cut into cubes for stew.

3. The Foreshank. This is the calf's front leg; it may be sold whole, boned and rolled or sliced into thick pieces. The meat, very flavorful and containing a large amount of gelatin, is braised or poached.

4 and 5. The Loin. The front part of the loin (4) is used to make rib chops, which can be boned or left with the rib bone. It also makes an excellent rib roast, which may or may not be arranged in a crown shape. Less meaty than the other section, it is a choice cut. The rear part of the loin (5) is also a choice cut, making a delicious roast, especially when it is boned (rolled loin). It can also be sliced into chops. The chops from both parts of the loin may be pan fried or braised.

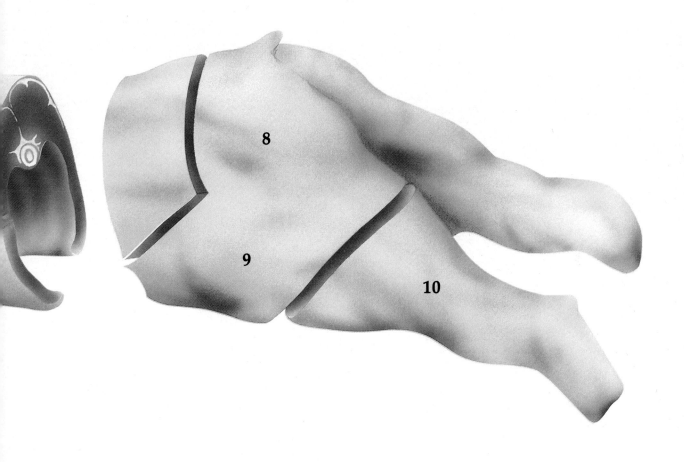

6. The Breast. Located just under the shoulder and loin, the breast is bony and contains fat and membranes. It can, however, be boned and rolled and used to make stuffed breast of veal, which may be roasted or braised. It also makes very high-quality ground veal.

7. The Flank. Located just behind the breast, the flank is used to make ground veal. It may also be cut into cubes, which make delicious kebabs.

8 and 9. The Round. This is divided into two sections: the upper part, or rump (8) and lower part, the round (9). The former makes a more tender roast, which may be roasted or braised, and can also be cut into blade chops. The latter can be boned and rolled and roasted or braised as well, and round steaks and veal cutlets (escallops) may also be taken from this section. Excellent veal cutlets, or escallops, and steaks can also be taken from the mid-section of the leg.

10. The Hind Shank. This section is also used to make stuffed roasts, which are usually braised.

Buying and Storing Veal

Buying Veal

The quality of a cooked dish depends on the quality of the ingredients used to prepare it. You cannot expect to turn a rancid piece of meat into a juicy, tasty roast. To avoid disappointment, you must know not only how to choose veal but also the best way to store it.

Veal is a special kind of meat, in that it always comes from a young animal. For this reason, you might expect it always to be tender. But unfortunately this is not the case; the tenderness will vary considerably according to the exact age of the calf and, to a lesser degree, the methods of preservation that have been used. If you want to buy meat from a very young calf—milk-fed veal, as it is called—choose pieces that are unmarbled and a pale pink color all over. Meat from calves that have been fed only milk is somewhat rare, so you may expect it to be rather expensive.

High-quality veal that comes from calves that are a bit older is also available commercially; they have started to eat grass and grain and are given powdered milk. The meat is a little less tender than that from a calf that has been fed only milk, but it is much more nutritious. Again, the color is a good indication of tenderness. Veal that is of a uniform light pink color and has little marbling comes from calves that have not been weaned. It is thus more tender than veal that is brighter pink in color and has more marbling and fat.

Whether the veal you buy is from very young or somewhat older calves, the fat must always be firm and ivory white. Avoid pieces in which the fat is yellow; they are not fresh and could be rancid. Also pay attention to the general appearance of the meat and bones; an oily looking piece with bones that are not porous may well give disappointing results.

As far as roasts are concerned, the most common come from the hind shank and shoulder. If you should choose the latter, remember that it is best to buy it boned because it is irregular in shape and the bone is in a position that makes the meat difficult to carve.

Storing Veal

Since high-quality veal is very tender and lean, it is also fragile; its taste could be severely affected if it is stored in an inappropriate way. For this reason, you should be very careful about the way you wrap the meat and how long you leave it in the refrigerator or freezer.

First, put meat that you have bought in the refrigerator as soon as possible. If you leave it until it reaches room temperature, bacteria will multiply. Remember, though, that the dry air circulating in the refrigerator causes meat to dry out quickly. Moreover, the oxygen circulates in a closed circuit and tends to cause the juices and fat to go rancid. It is for this reason essential to examine the original wrapping before refrigerating the meat. If the plastic has been torn in transport, change it—and certainly do not buy a package of meat if you see that it has been damaged.

As for freezing, opinions differ. Many feel that veal dries out and loses much of its flavor when frozen while others treat it as any other meat. It would be best, of course, to buy the meat just before cooking, but this is not always possible. So the second best thing is to freeze it, using the appropriate method in order to retain as much of its delicate taste as possible.

To do so, never freeze veal in its wrapping but rather in solid, tightly sealed containers or plastic bags—if possible, vacuum-sealed. The packaging should be airtight and watertight to prevent freezer burn. Remember never to refreeze a piece of veal that has been defrosted, even partially.

Consult the above chart for guidelines as to recommended storage times for different cuts of veal.

Storage Times for Veal

Cut	Refrigerator	Freezer*
Roasts	3 days	8 to 9 months
Loin and rib chops	2 days	3 to 4 months
Side ribs	2 days	3 to 4 months
Cubes	2 days	3 to 4 months
Escallops	24 hours	3 months
Ground veal	2 days	3 to 4 months
Offal (heart, liver, etc.)	1 to 2 days	3 months
Cooked veal	7 days	3 months

* Veal kept in the freezer must be put in airtight and watertight packages; otherwise, the cold dry air may cause freezer burn.

Defrosting Veal

Since you must be so careful in buying meat that is fresh and in wrapping it well before freezing, you might expect the rules for defrosting to be just as strict—otherwise, you might undo all your efforts. There is an ideal method for defrosting—you simply take the meat from the freezer and put it in the refrigerator until it is evenly defrosted. Sometimes, however, this is not possible. With the hectic pace of modern-day lifestyles, we cannot always plan in advance. The microwave oven offers an acceptable solution to this problem in that it allows you to speed up the defrosting process considerably. You can defrost the meat evenly, as long as you keep a few basic principles in mind and monitor the defrosting process.

Defrosting Roasts

With large pieces of meat such as roasts, you must avoid allowing some parts of the meat to start to cook while other parts are still frozen. The meat should lose as little juice as possible, otherwise, it would lose a great deal of its flavor. This point is particularly important for veal as it is very lean, not having much fat to start with. Take these three steps to obtain perfect results:

1. Put a rack or an upside-down plate in a large dish and stand the meat on it. The meat will then not come into contact with the juice that seeps out. Because liquids attract the microwaves, any parts of the meat standing in the juice would begin to cook before the center of the roast is defrosted.

2. After the first defrosting cycle, feel the meat and cover

any defrosted parts with aluminum foil (the bony parts and ends, especially). The microwaves will then be evenly distributed throughout the entire roast.

3. Divide the total time required for defrosting in the microwave into several short periods and allow a standing time equal to one quarter of the total defrosting time in between.

Defrosting Ground Veal

The method you choose for defrosting ground veal will depend on how you have frozen it—in a ring dish or a package. The ring shape is perfectly suited to defrosting in a microwave because the energy of the microwaves is more concentrated toward the outside of the dish. Since the center of the dish is empty, the power will be distributed equally. No special precautions are needed, except for the standing times between defrosting periods, as for roasts.

If the meat has been frozen in a package, unwrap it before defrosting or, it this is not possible, put it through a very short defrosting cycle, just enough to allow you to remove the wrapping. Then put it in a dish in the microwave for a first defrosting cycle. At the end of this cycle, scrape off any defrosted meat and break the rest into pieces with a fork. Put it in the oven for a second defrosting cycle and, again, remove any defrosted meat. If less than 450 grams (1 lb) is still frozen, simply let the meat stand for 10 minutes; but if there is more put it back for a final cycle.

Defrosting Guide*

Cut	Defrosting Time at 50%	Defrosting Time at 25%
Roasts	10 to 15 min/kg (5 to 7 min/lb)	17 to 19 min/kg (8 to 9 min/lb)
Loin and rib chops	6 to 10 min/kg (3 to 5 min/lb)	14 to 17 min/kg (6 to 8 min/lb)
Cubes	6 to 10 min/kg (3 to 5 min/lb)	14 to 17 min/kg (6 to 8 min/lb)
Escallops	6 to 10 min/kg (3 to 5 min/lb)	14 to 17 min/kg (6 to 8 min/lb)
Ground veal	6 to 10 min/kg (3 to 5 min/lb)	10 to 17 min/kg (5 to 8 min/lb)

* Don't forget to divide the defrosting time into two or three periods in the microwave oven with periods of standing time equal to a quarter of the total defrosting time in between defrosting periods.

Consult the above chart for recommended defrosting times for different cuts of veal.

Defrosting Escallops

To defrost escallops, simply unwrap them and put them on a bacon rack. Divide the defrosting time in two and turn the scallops over when they are half defrosted.

Ground veal that has been frozen in a tubular mold or ring dish can be defrosted easily and evenly in the microwave.

Cooking Veal

As we know, meat cooks quickly in a microwave oven. We also know that veal is a very tender but not very juicy meat that should not be cooked at too high a power level. Some might conclude that veal is not suited for cooking in a microwave oven and that it will take much trial and error to obtain satisfactory results. It is true that it requires special care, but there is no reason to worry unduly. As with other meats, cooking times are related to the cut of meat, its weight and, of course, the power level at which it is cooked. The temperature of the meat at the time it is put into the oven is also important, as is the water, fat and bone content. These factors are taken into account in the accompanying chart. Just follow the cooking times given, and you'll have a dish that will satisfy even the most discriminating gourmet.

Characteristics of Veal

Veal is a very delicate, fragile meat that owes its tenderness to its thin fibers rather than to its fat content. You must be careful not to cook it at too high a power level or for too long, or it will be dry and tough. The risk is all the greater since it is lean, has little marbling and produces only a small amount of juice in cooking. It is important to follow the instructions in the recipes for power levels and cooking times. When in doubt, cook for less time. You can always put it back in the oven if it isn't quite done, but

Cooking Times for Veal

Cut	Power Level	Cooking Time
Cubes, braised	50%	66 to 77 min/kg (30 to 35 min/lb)
Loin and rib chops	70%	10 to 15 min/kg (5 to 7 min/lb)
Escallops 1 or 2	100%	6 to 8 min
3 or 4	100%	7 to 9 min
Roasts Medium	50%	33 min/kg (15 min/lb)
Well done	50%	35 to 37 min/kg (16 to 17 min/lb)
Ground veal	100%	8 to 14 min/kg (4 to 6 min/lb)

if it is dried out there is nothing you can do.

You can prevent small cuts such as escallops from drying out by using butter, by breading or serving them with a sauce. Also, be careful how you place them in the cooking dish or they might cook unevenly. Place the escallops toward the outer edge of the dish.

There are precise rules for cooking roasts as well. Because a cut of this size takes much longer to cook and because its surface may dry out from being exposed to the microwaves for so long, it must be protected. You can lard it by making slits in the meat and inserting strips of fat into them, or you can bard it by placing strips of veal or pork fat across the surface of the meat. The roast may also be prevented from drying out by coating it with breadcrumbs or a glaze. Whatever method you choose, remember that a roast of veal must be basted frequently during cooking.

Ideally, the roast should be at room temperature when you put it in the oven.

You can prevent the surface of the roast of veal from drying out by coating it with breadcrumbs.

A roast of veal will not dry out if you bard it, that is, if you cover the surface with strips of veal or pork fat.

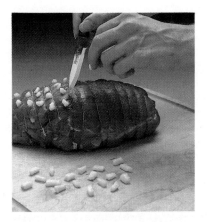

You can also prevent if from drying out by larding—making slits in the meat and inserting small pieces of fat into them.

MICROTIPS

Storing Calf's Liver
Ideally, calf's liver should be eaten as soon as possible after purchasing it, before it loses any of its nutritional value. It should not be refrigerated for more than two days. The best way to freeze slices of liver is to roll them up into compact packages. In this way, the microwaves will be more effective when it comes time to defrost.

Arranging Cuts of Veal in the Oven

Cooking veal in the microwave oven poses no problem as long as you cook it evenly. So with chops, escallops and roasts, pay particular attention to how you arrange the meat in the oven. By following a few simple steps, you can avoid the disappointment you will inevitably feel if you end up with a piece of meat half of which is uncooked and the other half dried out.

Loin and Rib Chops

To cook chops and ribs, place them on a rack which has been set in another suitable dish. Since the meat next to the bone tends to cook more quickly in a microwave and the food placed toward the outside attracts the most energy, be sure to put the parts with the least meat near the center. In this way, you are taking advantage of these two special characteristics of microwave cooking and your meal will be evenly cooked.

It is also important to divide the total cooking time into two periods and to turn the meat over at the end of the first period. If you are cooking six chops at once, rearrange them halfway through the cooking time, moving the chops in the center of the dish to the outer edge.

Escallops

Escallops are thin and the lean, tender meat requires a very short cooking time. Nevertheless, divide the cooking time in two and turn them over halfway through, just as you would do for chops. And again, if you are cooking several escallops at once, move any that are in the center to the outside at the same time. Like chops, escallops should be cooked on a rack so that they don't come into contact with the juice that seeps out.

Roasts

Since most roasts are cooked in their own juices in a covered dish, it is not necessary to use a rack. You will obtain the best results, however, if you place the part with the most fat on the bottom of the dish. It is always better to cover those parts with the least meat (the end, where there is a bone, for example) or those that are most exposed to the microwaves with aluminum foil.

Roast Loin of Veal, page 22

Veal Parmesan, page 42

Veal Cordon Bleu, page 45

Testing Veal for Doneness

Roast of veal is generally served medium or well done. It is difficult to tell how cooked it is just by touching the meat with a fork or knife because even when it is cooked to the medium point, it still feels firm to the touch due to its low fat content.

The best way to test for doneness is with a meat thermometer. At the end of the cooking time, take the roast out of the oven and insert the thermometer into the meat so that it is at least 2.5 cm (1 inch) away from the bone. If the thermometer indicates that the inside has reached 71°C (160°F), the roast is well done. Cover it with aluminum foil and let it stand for 10 minutes. The internal temperature will rise to approximately 74°C (165°F).

Carve one slice from the roast and check the color; if it is partially pink and partially brown, it is medium.

A roast is well done when the meat on the inside is uniformly brown.

There is a second method, just as simple as the first: carve a slice off the roast and check the color. The roast is medium if the inside is partially pink and partially brown and well done if it is uniformly brown.

MICROTIPS

To Rid the Oven of Cooking Odors

Sometimes lamb, especially the more fatty cuts, will leave a stubborn odor in the oven after cooking. It is easy to get rid of the odor; simply mix one cup of water with the zest and juice of a lemon in a small bowl. Heat the bowl in the oven at 100% for 3 minutes. Then wipe the inside of the oven with a cloth dampened with the same lemon and water mixture. Done!

Using an Earthenware Casserole Dish

There is no problem in using an earthenware casserole dish to cook veal or lamb in the microwave. But you must soak it in water for 15 minutes before using it; otherwise, it will absorb the juices from the food you are cooking. Afterwards, do not wash the dish with detergent, because it will absorb the taste of soap. Instead, scrub it with salt and rinse carefully with very hot water.

Roast Loin of Veal

Level of Difficulty	
Preparation Time	15 minutes
Cost per Serving	$ $ $
Number of Servings	10
Nutritional Value	300 calories 44.3 protein 5.8 mg iron
Food Exchanges	4 oz meat 1 fat exchange
Cooking Time	33 min/kg (15 min/lb) + 4 min
Standing Time	10 min
Power Level	50%, 100%
Write Your Cooking Time Here	

Ingredients

1 1.8 kg (4 lb) loin roast of veal
8 to 10 slices of bacon, 2 of them cut into pieces
pepper to taste
rosemary to taste
1 package onion soup mix
2 celery stalks, chopped
2 carrots, chopped
2 onions, cut in wedges
125 mL (1/2 cup) white wine
salt and pepper to taste

Method

— Make slits in the roast and insert the pieces of bacon into them.
— Sprinkle the roast with pepper and rosemary; cover with the uncut bacon slices and attach them firmly.
— Place the roast in a dish and sprinkle the package of onion soup mix over it.
— Cover and cook at 50% for 33 min/kg (15 min/lb). Halfway through the cooking time, turn the roast over and add the celery, carrots and onions.
— Give the dish a half-turn once during the last stage of cooking.
— When done, remove the roast and vegetables from the dish, let stand for 10 minutes and deglaze the dish with the white wine.
— Heat the mixture for 2 minutes at 100%, then strain and season. For a thicker sauce, add 15 mL (1 tablespoon) cornstarch mixed with 30 mL (2 tablespoons) cold water and cook at 100% for 1 or 2 minutes longer or until the sauce thickens.

Simple, yet flavorful ingredients are the basis for this extraordinarily tasty recipe.

Lard the roast by making slits in the surface and inserting pieces of bacon into them.

Once the roast has been sprinkled with spices and larded, pour the contents of a package of onion soup mix over it.

Rolled Roast of Veal

Level of Difficulty	
Preparation Time	15 min
Cost per Serving	$ $ $
Number of Servings	10
Nutritional Value	253 calories 40.4 protein 5.5 mg iron
Food Exchanges	4 oz meat
Cooking Time	33 min/kg (15 min/lb) + 3 min
Standing Time	10 min
Power Level	100%, 50%
Write Your Cooking Time Here	

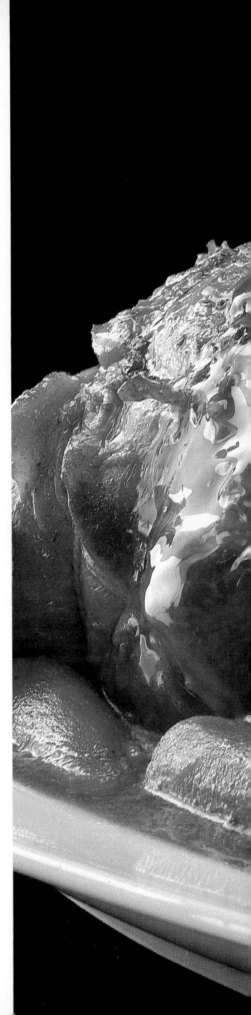

Ingredients
1 1.8 kg (4 lb) veal roast, boned and rolled
1 clove garlic, cut in two
pepper to taste
2 onions, sliced
5 mL (1 teaspoon) sage
30 mL (2 tablespoons) brown sugar
250 mL (1 cup) dry white wine
15 mL (1 tablespoon) parsley, chopped
10 small carrots

Method
— Rub the roast with the garlic and sprinkle with pepper; place in a cooking bag.
— In a bowl, combine all other ingredients, except the carrots.
— Cook for 2 to 3 minutes at 100% and pour the mixture into the bag with the veal.
— Place the bag in a dish and close it, leaving room for steam to escape.
— Roast at 50% for 33 min/kg (15 min/lb). Add the carrots halfway through the cooking time and give the dish a half-turn twice during the cooking time.
— Let stand for 10 minutes.

Roast Veal Shoulder with Cabbage

Level of Difficulty	🍴
Preparation Time	15 min
Cost per Serving	$ $ $
Number of Servings	10
Nutritional Value	410 calories 40.4 g protein 5.4 mg iron
Food Exchanges	4 oz meat 1 vegetable exchange 2 fat exchanges
Cooking Time	33 min/kg (15 min/lb) + 3 min
Standing Time	10 min
Power Level	100%, 50%
Write Your Cooking Time Here	

Ingredients
1 veal shoulder, boned and rolled
115 g (4 oz) salt pork
2 mL (1/2 teaspoon) pepper
60 mL (4 tablespoons) oil
15 mL (1 tablespoon) flour
250 mL (1 cup) hot water
2 medium onions, cut into pieces
2 carrots, cut in strips
2 small cabbages, cut in quarters

Method
— Lard the veal shoulder by making slits in the surface and inserting pieces of the pork fat into them; sprinkle with the pepper.
— Preheat a browning dish for 7 minutes at 100%; add the oil and heat for 30 seconds at 100%.
— Sear the roast, remove from the dish and set aside.
— Add the flour to the dish, mix well and add the hot water; cook for 2 to 3 minutes at 100%.

Roast Veal Shoulder with Cabbage

An ideal dish for a full house. First, assemble the ingredients required.

Lard the shoulder roast by making slits in the surface and filling them with pieces of pork fat to add moisture during the cooking period.

Sear the roast in oil in the preheated browning dish.

Turn the roast over halfway through the cooking time so that it will be evenly cooked.

Add the carrots and cabbage and cover again before continuing to cook.

Give the dish a half-turn during the last stage of cooking.

— Put the roast back in the dish and add the onions.
— Cover and cook at 50% for 33 min/kg (15 min/lb). Halfway through the cooking time, add the carrots and cabbage and turn the roast over.
— Cover again and continue cooking at 50%, giving the dish a half-turn once during this last cooking stage.
— Let stand for 10 minutes before slicing and serving.

Sauces for Veal and Lamb

All serious cooks agree that to treat food properly, you must have a good repertoire of sauces to call on when needed. And gourmets and food lovers all say that nothing enhances the flavor of a piece of meat more than a sauce that blends perfectly with it. Everyone seems to agree, then, on the importance of sauces.

Some Sauces for Veal

A lean and delicate meat, veal goes especially well with light sauces—those having a white wine base, for example. When you cook a roast, you can make an excellent sauce by removing the fat from the bottom of the dish and deglazing it with white wine. Mustard and cream, for instance, may then be added and reduced with the cooking juices and the wine to produce a smooth, tasty sauce.

Veal chops, like steaks, can be served with a sauce made by deglazing with red wine and adding chopped green onions.

If you lard and braise a veal roast with a number of vegetables, you can glaze the roast with the broth after reducing it. You can also use the broth to make an onion sauce, which is delicious with all cuts of veal. Just brown the onions, sprinkle them with a bit of flour, add a touch of vinegar and then blend in the broth.

Veal can also be served with such traditional sauces as béchamel and other white sauces, béarnaise sauce and sweet-and-sour cream sauce. Other ingredients used in making sauces to enhance the flavor of veal include cranberries, celery, red currants, oranges, apples, tomatoes, horseradish, beer, calvados, cognac and port.

Some Sauces for Lamb

It there is one sauce that goes well with lamb, it's mint sauce. It is very popular because it has a sharp taste and a strong enough odor to mask the strong taste and aroma that lamb fat sometimes gives to the meat. (It is really only older lamb, from which the fat has not been properly trimmed, that has this strong flavor.) Nevertheless, over the years, mint sauce has become the traditional companion for a leg of lamb.

A number of quite spicy sauces are also served with lamb, such as harissa sauce, which comes from the Mediterranean, where lamb is a favorite.

You can use lamb broth as the base for several sauces by thickening it with roux and adding capers, small turnips sautéed in butter, or finely chopped carrots and onions, cooked in butter until golden brown.

Aniseed, cranberries, cheese and tomatoes constitute some other ingredients used in sauces for lamb. And traditional sauces, such as white (béchamel) sauce, are also well suited to lamb.

When it comes to choosing a sauce for lamb or veal, remember that it is intended to bring out the meat's qualities and complement its character. For this reason, strong sauces should not be served with delicately flavored dishes—in other words, light, subtle sauces should be served with veal while stronger sauces are quite suitable for lamb.

Veal Casserole

Level of Difficulty	
Preparation Time	15 min
Cost per Serving	$ $
Number of Servings	6
Nutritional Value	324 calories 35 g protein 4.8 mg iron
Food Exchanges	3 oz meat 2 fat exchanges
Cooking Time	1 h 10 min
Standing Time	3 min
Power Level	100%, 70%
Write Your Cooking Time Here	

Ingredients

900 g (2 lb) veal, cut into 2.5 cm (1 in) cubes
45 mL (3 tablespoons) butter
2 onions, finely sliced
5 mL (1 teaspoon) salt
2 mL (1/2 teaspoon) pepper
1 284 mL (10 oz) can condensed cream of celery soup
1 mL (1/4 teaspoon) Tabasco sauce
50 mL (1/4 cup) red wine
250 mL (1 cup) sour cream

Method

— Preheat a browning dish for 7 minutes at 100%; add the butter and heat for 30 seconds at 100%.
— Sear the veal cubes, remove from the dish and set aside.
— Add the onions, cover and cook at 100% for 2 to 3 minutes, stirring once.
— Add the salt, half the pepper, cream of celery soup, Tabasco sauce and red wine; cover and cook at 100% for 3 to 4 minutes, stirring at one-minute intervals.
— Add the veal cubes, reduce the power level to 70% and cook for 30 minutes.
— Stir and continue cooking at 70% for 25 to 30 minutes, or until the veal is tender.
— Blend in the sour cream and remaining pepper.
— Increase the power level to 100%, cover and cook 2 to 3 minutes, stirring each minute.
— Let stand for 3 minutes before serving.

A recipe that will surely please the palates of those who enjoy veal with a creamy sauce. First, assemble the ingredients needed.

After searing the veal cubes in butter in the preheated browning dish, cook the onions.

Before the final stage of cooking blend in the sour cream.

Veal Rump Roast with Apples

Level of Difficulty	🍴🍴
Preparation Time	15 min
Cost per Serving	$ $
Number of Servings	12
Nutritional Value	402 calories 40.4 g protein 5.5 mg iron
Food Exchanges	4 1/2 oz meat 1/2 fat exchange 1 fruit exchange
Cooking Time	33 min/kg (15 min/lb) + 12 min
Standing Time	None
Power Level	100%, 50%
Write Your Cooking Time Here	

Ingredients
1 2.25 kg (5 lb) veal rump roast
30 mL (2 tablespoons) oil
375 mL (1-1/2 cups) apple juice
1 medium onion, diced
15 mL (1 tablespoon) marinating spice, wrapped in cheesecloth
10 mL (2 teaspoons) salt
1 mL (1/4 teaspoon) pepper
5 green apples, cut in quarters
45 mL (3 tablespoons) cornstarch
75 mL (1/3 cup) cold water

Method
— Preheat a browning dish for 7 minutes at 100%; add the oil and heat for 30 seconds at 100%.
— Sear the roast, remove from the dish and set aside.
— Add the apple juice, onion, marinating spice, salt and pepper to the browning dish.
— Bring to a boil by cooking the mixture for 4 to 5 minutes at 100%.
— Add the roast and cover the dish; cook at 50% for 33 min/kg (15 min/lb), making sure to turn the roast over every 20 minutes.
— When the cooking time is up, remove the roast and the marinating spice, and add the apples to the liquid.
— Cover and cook at 100% for 5 minutes, stirring once.
— Add the cornstarch, dissolved in the water, and cook at 100% for 1 to 2 minutes or until the sauce thickens, stirring every minute.

Wrap the marinating spice in cheesecloth to make it easier to remove before serving.

After searing the roast and removing it from the dish, add the apple juice, onion and seasonings.

Turn the roast over every 20 minutes during the cooking time.

Aromatics and Spices for Veal and Lamb

Veal and lamb are choice meats and it is absolutely essential to emphasize their qualities. Although veal is not very juicy, it is extremely tender and has a subtle flavor; to enhance this flavor use a discreet type of seasoning— and not too much. Lamb has a more marked flavor so you can go stronger on the seasoning. In both cases, however, aromatics and spices only play a supporting role; the star will always be the meat with which they are served.

Herbs such as thyme, marjoram and bay leaves are well-known aromatics, but we sometimes forget that numerous vegetables, such as fennel, onions, carrots, celery and most root vegetables are aromatics as well. It is impossible, of course, to give hard and fast rules about seasoning; it will always be a matter of individual taste. But we can point out some of the aromatics most frequently used in the most successful dishes.

Because of its delicate flavor, veal should be seasoned with sweet aromatics—aromatic vegetables such as celery, carrots, fennel, leeks, garlic, shallots and onions are frequently used. As far as herbs are concerned, thyme, bay, savory and parsley seem to be the favorites of many cooks. Poached veal may be seasoned with a *bouquet garni,* and spices such as nutmeg, pepper and allspice are also often used.

Slices and zest of lemon are delicious with veal. An extraordinary *gremolata,* a garnish for braised veal, is made by mixing chopped garlic, chopped parsley and lemon or orange zest.

The more marked flavor of lamb is enhanced with stronger herbs, such as mint or aniseed, or with more generous doses of thyme, marjoram, parsley, savory, tarragon and oregano. Rosemary, however, is the herb that is most often associated with lamb.

Garlic, scallions, onions, cayenne pepper, juniper berries, capers and pepper also give lamb and mutton dishes interesting flavors. As with veal, lemon also adds an interesting touch to certain lamb recipes.

Calf's Liver

Level of Difficulty	¶¶¶
Preparation Time	10 min
Cost per Serving	$ $
Number of Servings	4
Nutritional Value	375 calories 35 g protein 15.8 mg iron
Food Exchanges	4 oz meat 1 vegetable exchange 1 fat exchange
Cooking Time	9 min
Standing Time	None
Power Level	100%, 70%
Write Your Cooking Time Here	

Ingredients
4 large slices of calf's liver
125 mL (1/2 cup) flour
salt and pepper to taste
5 mL (1 teaspoon) oil
30 mL (2 tablespoons) butter
2 medium onions, sliced
30 mL (2 tablespoons) wine vinegar
15 mL (1 tablespoon) parsley, chopped
15 mL (1 tablespoon) lemon juice

Method
— Preheat a browning dish for 7 minutes at 100%.
— In the meantime, combine the flour, salt and pepper; dredge the liver and set aside.
— Add the oil and butter to the browning dish and heat for 30 seconds at 100%.
— Sear the liver slices on both sides.
— Reduce the power level to 70% and cook uncovered for 3 to 4 minutes, giving the dish a half-turn after 2 minutes.
— Remove the slices of liver and set aside.
— Add the onions and cook at 100% for 3 to 4 minutes, stirring after 2 minutes; add the wine vinegar, parsley and lemon juice.
— Cook for 1 minute at 100%. Garnish the liver with the onion mixture before serving.

Calf's liver is easy to prepare and always enjoyed. First assemble the ingredients.

Dredge the slices of liver in the seasoned flour before cooking.

Sear the liver in a preheated browning dish in a mixture of oil and butter.

Braised Veal Shank

Level of Difficulty	
Preparation Time	20 min
Cost per Serving	$
Number of Servings	6
Nutritional Value	270 calories 27.8 g protein 4.1 mg iron
Food Exchanges	3 oz meat 1 vegetable exchange 2 fat exchanges
Cooking Time	35 min
Standing Time	5 min
Power Level	100%, 70%, 90%
Write Your Cooking Time Here	

Ingredients
6 pieces of veal shank, 5 cm (2 in) thick
125 mL (1/2 cup) flour, browned
75 mL (1/3 cup) oil
2 medium onions, finely chopped
125 mL (1/2 cup) celery, diced
125 mL (1/2 cup) mushrooms, sliced
45 mL (3 tablespoons) parsley, chopped
1 large carrot, grated
2 cloves garlic, finely chopped
5 mL (1 teaspoon) oregano
1 540 mL (19 oz) can whole tomatoes, drained
125 mL (1/2 cup) chicken broth
2 mL (1/2 teaspoon) sugar

Method
— Preheat a browning dish for 7 minutes at 100%.
— In the meantime, dredge the shank pieces in the flour, shaking off any excess.
— Pour the oil into the dish and heat for 30 seconds at 100%.
— Sear the pieces of shank.
— Reduce the power level to 70%, cover the dish and cook for 4 to 5 minutes, giving the dish a half-turn after 3 minutes.
— Add all the other ingredients, making sure to leave the tomatoes whole.
— Increase the power level to 90%, cover and cook for 25 to 30 minutes or until the meat is done, giving the dish a half-turn after 15 minutes. For a thicker sauce, remove the meat when done and add cornstarch dissolved in a little water to the liquid. Cook at 100%, stirring frequently, making sure not to break up the tomatoes.
— Let stand for 5 minutes before serving.

This recipe, rich in vegetables, will please even the most demanding tastes. First assemble the ingredients required to prepare it.

While the browning dish is being preheated, dredge the pieces of shank in flour that has been browned in the microwave.

Veal with Stewed Fruit

Level of Difficulty	◼
Preparation Time	10 min*
Cost per Serving	$ $ $
Number of Servings	4
Nutritional Value	412 calories 42.7 g protein 6.5 mg iron
Food Exchanges	4 oz meat 1 fat exchange 1-1/2 fruit exchanges
Cooking Time	20 min
Standing Time	None
Power Level	100%, 70%
Write Your Cooking Time Here	

* The meat must marinate for at least 1 hour before cooking.

Ingredients
2 veal tenderloins, weighing
675 g (1-1/2 lbs) in total
30 mL (2 tablespoons) Dijon
mustard
30 mL (2 tablespoons) oil
salt and pepper to taste
150 mL (2/3 cup) toasted
sesame seeds
stewed fruit, enough for 4
servings

Method
— In a bowl, combine the
  Dijon mustard, oil, salt
  and pepper and whisk
  well.
— Brush the tenderloins with
  the mixture and allow to
  marinate for 1 hour.
— Preheat a browning dish
  for 7 minutes at 100%,
  and sear the veal.
— Reduce the power level to
  70% and cook for 10
  minutes.
— Give the dish a half-turn
  and continue to cook at
  70% for 8 to 10 minutes,
  or until the meat is
  cooked.
— Slice the veal into
  medallions and sprinkle
  with sesame seeds; serve
  with stewed fruit.

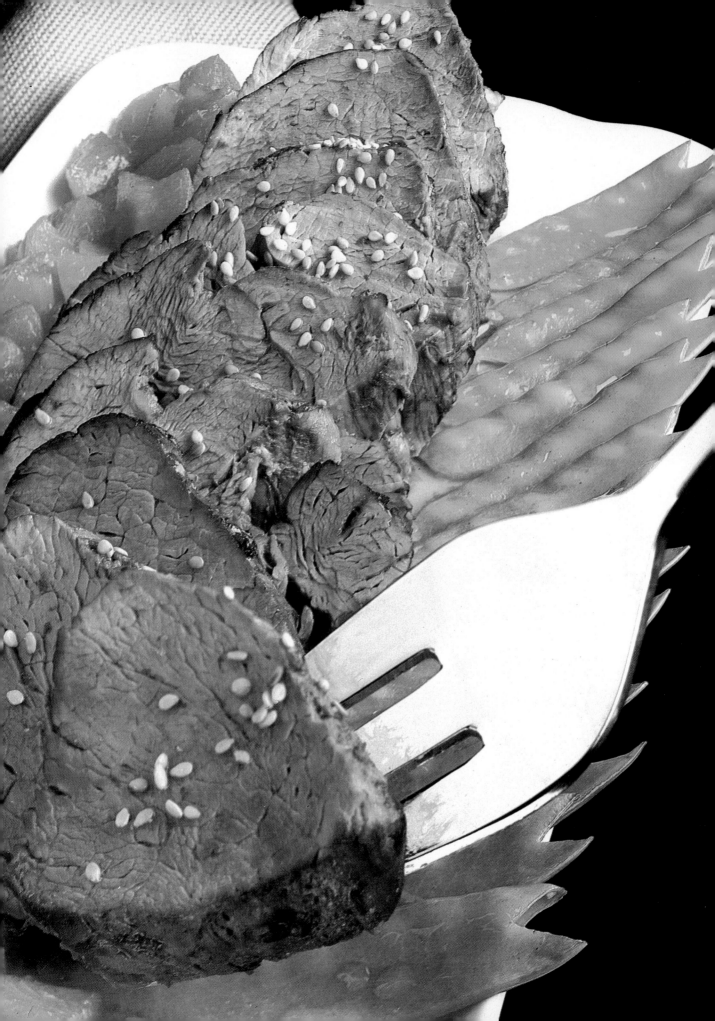

Paupiettes of Veal

Level of Difficulty	🍴🍴
Preparation Time	20 min*
Cost per Serving	$ $ $
Number of Servings	5
Nutritional Value	371 calories 40.4 g protein 5.2 mg iron
Food Exchanges	4-1/2 oz meat 3 fat exchanges 1/4 bread exchange
Cooking Time	57 min
Standing Time	5 min
Power Level	100%, 70%
Write Your Cooking Time Here	

* The sauce must be left to stand for 30 minutes to allow the flavor to be fully developed before the wine is added and the paupiettes are cooked in it.

Ingredients
10 veal escallops
250 mL (1 cup) bread, crusts removed
50 mL (1/4 cup) milk
115 g (4 oz) ground veal
115 g (4 ox) ground pork
tarragon, basil and thyme to taste
1 clove garlic, crushed
salt and pepper to taste
30 mL (2 tablespoons) butter

Sauce:
50 mL (1/4 cup) butter
1 carrot, finely sliced
3 green onions, finely sliced
1 clove garlic, chopped
1 onion, finely chopped
50 mL (1/4 cup) flour
500 mL (2 cups) chicken broth
1 bay leaf
5 mL (1 teaspoon) thyme
5 mL (1 teaspoon) parsley, chopped
125 mL (1/2 cup) white wine

Method
— To make the sauce, melt the butter for 1 minute at 100% and then add the vegetables and garlic.
— Cover and cook at 100% for 4 to 5 minutes, stirring once.
— Sprinkle with the flour, stir again and add the chicken broth and seasoning.
— Cover and cook at 100% for 25 to 30 minutes, stirring once.
— Let the mixture stand to settle for 30 minutes, then

strain the broth and set
aside.
— Meanwhile, to make the
paupiettes, soak the bread
in the milk.
— Combine the ground veal
and pork, tarragon, basil,
thyme, garlic, salt and
pepper, and then add the
bread.
— Mix the stuffing well, until
it is of an even
consistency, and then
divide it into 10 equal
portions.
— Set one portion on each
slice of veal, roll up

jelly-roll fashion and
fasten with a toothpick;
set aside.
— Add the white wine to the
cooled sauce and heat for
4 to 5 minutes at 100%,
stirring once; set aside.
— Preheat a browning dish
for 7 minutes at 100%,
add the butter and heat
for 30 seconds at 100%.
— Sear the stuffed
paupiettes.
— Add the sauce, cover,
reduce the power level to
70% and cook for 7
minutes.

— Change the position of the
paupiettes, moving those
in the center to the outside
and vice-versa.
— Continue cooking at 70%
for 7 to 9 minutes.
— Let stand for 5 minutes
before serving.

Veal Parmesan

Level of Difficulty	▯▮▯
Preparation Time	15 min
Cost per Serving	$ $
Number of Servings	6
Nutritional Value	360 calories 32.1 g protein 4 mg iron
Food Exchanges	4 oz meat 1-1/2 fat exchanges
Cooking Time	16 min
Standing Time	3 min
Power Level	100%, 70%, 90%
Write Your Cooking Time Here	

Ingredients
6 veal escallops
15 mL (1 tablespoon) milk
1 egg, beaten
50 mL (1/4 cup) fine breadcrumbs
50 mL (1/4 cup) Parmesan cheese, grated
salt and pepper to taste
45 mL (3 tablespoons) butter
250 mL (1 cup) Italian-style tomato sauce
250 mL (1 cup) mozzarella cheese, grated
paprika to taste

Method
— Add the milk to the beaten egg; combine the breadcrumbs and Parmesan cheese, and season.
— Bread the escallops by dipping in the egg and milk mixture and then coating with the breadcrumb/Parmesan mixture.
— Preheat a browning dish for 7 minutes at 100%; add the butter and heat for 30 seconds at 100%.
— Sear the escallops, reduce

Veal Parmesan

This Italian-style dish is extremely popular. First assemble the ingredients needed.

To bread the escallops, first dip them into the egg and milk mixture.

Then coat the escallops with the seasoned Parmesan and breadcrumb mixture.

Sear the escallops in butter in a preheated browning dish.

Pour the tomato sauce into another dish and place the escallops on top.

Cover with the grated mozzarella and sprinkle with paprika before the final stage of cooking.

the power level to 70% and cook for 6 minutes.
— Pour the tomato sauce into another dish and place the escallops on top of it.

— Cover with the mozzarella and sprinkle with paprika.
— Raise the power level to 90% and cook for 8 to 10 minutes or until done,

giving the dish a half-turn halfway through the cooking time.
— Let stand for 3 minutes before serving.

Veal Cordon Bleu

Ingredients
4 veal escallops
4 slices cooked ham
4 slices cheddar or
Emmenthal cheese

50 mL (1/4 cup) flour
2 eggs, beaten
50 mL (1/4 cup) breadcrumbs
pepper to taste
45 mL (3 tablespoons) butter

Level of Difficulty	🍴🍴
Preparation Time	20 min
Cost per Serving	$ $
Number of Servings	4
Nutritional Value	422 calories 39 g protein 4 mg iron
Food Exchanges	4 oz meat 2 fat exchanges 1/2 bread exchange
Cooking Time	9 min
Standing Time	3 min
Power Level	100%, 70%
Write Your Cooking Time Here	

Method
— Place the escallops between two sheets of waxed paper and flatten by pounding them.
— Place a slice of ham and a slice of cheese on each one.
— Roll the escallops up, jelly-roll fashion, and fasten with toothpicks.
— Dredge them in the flour, shaking off any excess; dip into the beaten eggs and then coat with the breadcrumbs; season with pepper.
— Preheat a browning dish for 7 minutes at 100%, add the butter and heat for 30 seconds at 100%.
— Sear the escallops, reduce the power level to 70% and cook for 6 to 9 minutes or until done. Turn the escallops over halfway through the cooking time.
— Let stand for 3 minutes before serving.

Wiener Schnitzel

Level of Difficulty	🍴🍴🍴
Preparation Time	20 min
Cost per Serving	$ $
Number of Servings	6
Nutritional Value	294 calories 28.1 g protein 3.9 mg iron
Food Exchanges	3 oz meat 1/2 bread exchange
Cooking Time	5 min
Standing Time	None
Power Level	90%
Write Your Cooking Time Here	

Ingredients
6 large veal escallops, 5 mm
(1/4 in) thick
75 mL (1/3 cup) flour
6 mL (1-1/4 teaspoons) salt
2 eggs, beaten
125 mL (1/2 cup)
breadcrumbs
45 mL (3 tablespoons)
parsley, chopped
6 lemon slices

Method
— Place the escallops
between two sheets of
waxed paper and pound
until they are 3 mm (1/8
in) thick.
— Combine the flour and salt
and dredge the escallops.
— Dip them into the beaten
eggs and then coat with
the breadcrumbs.
— Place the escallops on a
bacon rack and cook at
90% for 4 to 5 minutes, or
until done, giving the rack
a half-turn halfway
through the cooking time.
— Sprinkle with parsley and
garnish with the lemon
slices before serving.

*This easy-to-prepare recipe calls
for ingredients that you're sure
to have on hand. It's useful to
assemble them before
beginning.*

Coat the escallops with breadcrumbs after dipping them in the beaten eggs.

Place the breaded escallops on a bacon rack and cook for 4 to 5 minutes at 90%.

Give the rack a half-turn halfway through the cooking time.

Veal Sauté Marengo

Level of Difficulty	🍴
Preparation Time	20 min
Cost per Serving	$ $
Number of Servings	6
Nutritional Value	329 calories 51.7 g protein 7.1 mg iron
Food Exchanges	4 oz meat 1 vegetable exchange 1-1/2 fat exchanges
Cooking Time	1 h 34 min
Standing Time	5 min
Power Level	100%, 50%
Write Your Cooking Time Here	

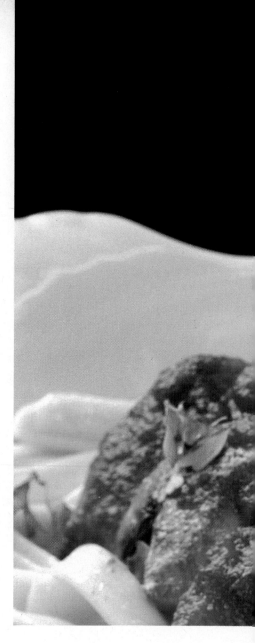

Ingredients
1.3 kg (3 lb) veal, cubed
50 mL (1/4 cup) oil
30 mL (2 tablespoons) flour
125 mL (1/2 cup) beef stock
250 mL (1 cup) tomato sauce
5 mL (1 teaspoon) salt
2 mL (1/2 teaspoon) pepper
5 mL (1 teaspoon) thyme
250 mL (1 cup) onion, diced
2 cloves garlic, finely sliced
15 mL (1 tablespoon) parsley, chopped
1 bay leaf
225 g (8 oz) mushrooms, sliced

Method
— Preheat a browning dish for 7 minutes at 100%; add the oil and heat for 30 seconds at 100%.
— Sear the cubes and sprinkle with the flour.
— Add the beef stock and tomato sauce, and cook at 100% for 3 to 4 minutes, stirring once.
— Add all the other ingredients except the mushrooms; reduce the power level to 50%, cover and cook for 40 minutes.
— Stir and continue to cook at 50% for 40 minutes.
— Stir once again, add the mushrooms; cover and continue to cook at 50% for 8 to 10 minutes, or until the meat is done.
— Let stand for 5 minutes before serving.

MICROTIPS

Barding a Roast of Veal

Veal is a very lean type of meat, with little marbling. It produces very little juice in cooking and tends to dry out if cooked for very long. But a roast of veal will remain tender if it is barded before cooking. To do so, cut large strips of veal or pork fat, 3 to 4 cm (approximately 1 to 1-1/2 inches) thick and then cut half of them into thin strips. Place the thin strips on top of the roast and put the ones around the four sides. Tie string around the roast to keep them in place.

Veal Galantine

Level of Difficulty	
Preparation Time	15 min
Cost per Serving	$
Number of Servings	10
Nutritional Value	76 calories 1.35 g protein 1.8 mg iron
Food Exchanges	1 oz meat
Cooking Time	1 h 10 min
Standing Time	None
Power Level	100%, 90%
Write Your Cooking Time Here	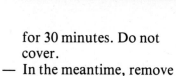

Ingredients
1 900 g to 1.3 kg (2 to 3 lb)
veal hind shank, lean
15 mL (1 tablespoon) salt
2 mL (1/2 teaspoon) pepper
750 mL (3 cups) water
1 carrot, grated
125 mL (1/2 cup) celery
leaves, chopped
1 large onion, finely chopped

Method
— Combine all the
  ingredients in a dish.
— Cover and cook for 10
  minutes at 100%.
— Stir, reduce the power
  level to 90%; cover again
  and cook for 20 to 30
  minutes, or until the meat
  is done.
— Remove the meat from the
  dish.
— Cook the broth at 100%
  for 30 minutes. Do not
  cover.
— In the meantime, remove
  the meat from the bone
  and place in a mold.
— Strain the broth and pour
  into the mold.
— Let cool before serving.

MICROTIPS

To Flatten Veal Escallops

Veal is a delicate meat and a certain amount of care must be taken in preparing escallops. Using the jagged side of a meat mallet to pound them would cause them to tear. Instead, use the smooth side of the mallet, making sure that you hit them with the blunt surface only—not at an angle because the corners of the mallet would pierce the escallops.

If you do not have a meat mallet, a small heavy frying pan may be used; simply hit them gently with the bottom of it.

Blanquette of Veal

Level of Difficulty	🍴
Preparation Time	20 min
Cost per Serving	$ $
Number of Servings	8
Nutritional Value	325 calories 41.4 g protein 6.04 mg iron
Food Exchanges	4 oz meat 1 vegetable exchange 1 fat exchange
Cooking Time	1 h 29 min
Standing Time	3 min
Power Level	70%, 50%
Write Your Cooking Time Here	

Ingredients
1.3 kg (3 lb) stewing veal, cubed
250 mL (1 cup) celery, diced
250 mL (1 cup) carrots, diced
2 cloves
1 bay leaf
125 mL (1/2 cup) dry vermouth
10 mL (2 teaspoons) salt
hot water
450 g (1 lb) small pearl onions, peeled
450 g (1 lb) button mushrooms
4 egg yolks, beaten
125 mL (1/2 cup) 35% cream

Method
— Prepare a *bouquet garni* by wrapping the celery, carrots, cloves and bay leaf in cheesecloth.
— Place the *bouquet garni* in a casserole and add the veal cubes, vermouth and salt. Add just enough hot water to cover the meat.
— Cover and cook at 70% for 30 minutes, skimming the surface periodically during the cooking time.
— Stir, reduce the power level to 50% and continue to cook for 30 minutes.
— Add the onions, cover once more and cook for 15 minutes at 50%.
— Stir and add the mushrooms.
— Cover and cook at 50% for 10 minutes or until the meat is tender.
— In a bowl, combine the egg yolks and cream, and add a little of the cooking liquid.
— Pour this mixture back into the casserole, stirring well to avoid lumps.
— Cook at 70% for 3 to 4 minutes, or until the sauce thickens, stirring each minute. Do not allow the sauce to boil.
— Let stand for 3 minutes and remove the *bouquet garni* before serving.

MICROTIPS

For Spaghetti Sauce That Is Less Fattening
People who watch the amount of fat they eat frequently choose spaghetti sauces without meat because they think they will ruin their diet by having the beef. Why not make your spaghetti sauce by using half hamburger, half ground veal?

Veal Fricassee

Level of Difficulty	🍴
Preparation Time	10 min
Cost per Serving	$ $
Number of Servings	4
Nutritional Value	243 calories 34.7 g protein 5.1 mg iron
Food Exchanges	3 oz meat 1 vegetable exchange
Cooking Time	40 min
Standing Time	5 min
Power Level	70%
Write Your Cooking Time Here	

Ingredients
450 g (1 lb) veal, cut into
2.5 cm (1 in) cubes
500 mL (2 cups) pearl onions,
peeled
75 mL (1/3 cup) water
75 mL (1/3 cup) tomato paste
45 mL (3 tablespoons) vinegar
45 mL (3 tablespoons) red
wine
2 cloves garlic, crushed
5 mL (1 teaspoon) brown
sugar
250 mL (1 cup) mushrooms,
sliced
30 mL (2 tablespoons) fresh
parsley, chopped

Method
— In a casserole, combine the
veal cubes, pearl onions,
water, tomato paste,
vinegar, red wine, garlic
and brown sugar. Mix
well.
— Cover and cook for 20
minutes at 70%.
— Stir and add a little more
water if the meat is drying
out.
— Cover again and continue
to cook at 70% for 10
minutes.
— Add the mushrooms,
cover again and cook at
70% for 7 to 10 minutes,
or until the meat is tender.
— Let stand for 5 minutes.
Sprinkle with parsley
before serving.

Although a traditional dish, veal fricassee is still a favorite. Here are the ingredients.

Combine all the ingredients, except the mushrooms and the parsley. Cover and cook.

Add the mushrooms before the final stage of cooking.

Veal Loaf

Level of Difficulty	
Preparation Time	15 min
Cost per Serving	$
Number of Servings	8
Nutritional Value	331 calories 29.5 g protein 4 mg iron
Food Exchanges	4 oz meat 1/4 milk exchange
Cooking Time	13 min
Standing Time	5 min
Power Level	100%, 50%
Write Your Cooking Time Here	

Ingredients
675 g (1-1/2 lb) ground veal
225 g (1/2 lb) ground ham
250 mL (1 cup) breadcrumbs
250 mL (1 cup) evaporated milk
2 eggs
juice of 1 lemon
zest of 1/4 lemon, grated
5 mL (1 teaspoon) salt
6 drops of Tabasco sauce
125 mL (1/2 cup) tomato juice
3 slices of bacon

Method
— Combine the ground veal and ham, mix well and set aside.
— Combine the breadcrumbs and evaporated milk; set aside to allow the breadcrumbs to soak up the milk.
— Beat the eggs and add the milk and breadcrumb mixture, the lemon juice and zest, salt, Tabasco sauce and tomato juice.
— Combine with the meat mixture and mix well.
— Pour the mixture into a loaf dish and place the 3 slices of bacon on top.
— Cover the two ends of the dish with aluminum foil and cook for 3 minutes at 100%.
— Give the dish a half-turn, reduce the power level to 50% and cook for 8 to 10 minutes or until done, giving the dish a half-turn and removing the foil halfway through the cooking time.
— Let stand for 5 minutes before serving.

MICROTIPS

shoulder roast is complex and irregular in shape, making it difficult to carve.

Shoulder Roast—A Good Choice

Most roasts of veal are taken from the shoulder of shank. If you buy a shoulder roast, it is best to choose one that is boned because the structure of an unboned

An Easy Glaze for Roast Veal

Veal is a very lean meat that produces little juice in cooking. Large roasts of veal are therefore frequently braised and the meat is basted often during cooking.

However, a roast should not be cooked in too much juice. A popular solution to the problem is to glaze the roast, which will to some extent seal the surface and keep it from drying out. There are several glazes that are ideal for veal, but the simplest is to coat the roast with orange marmalade or red currant jelly, both of which go well with veal.

Calf's Brains

Ingredients

4 calf's brains
750 mL (3 cups) cold water
30 mL (2 tablespoons) white vinegar
2 bay leaves
2 cloves garlic, chopped
5 mL (1 teaspoon) salt
5 mL (1 teaspoon) pepper
250 mL (1 cup) hot water
45 mL (3 tablespoons) butter
15 mL (1 tablespoon) parsley

Level of Difficulty	🍴🍴
Preparation Time	20 min*
Cost per Serving	$
Number of Servings	4
Nutritional Value	217 calories 11.7 g protein 2.7 mg iron
Food Exchanges	2.5 oz meat 2 fat exchanges
Cooking Time	8 min
Standing Time	2 min
Power Level	100%
Write Your Cooking Time Here	

Method

— Soak the brains for 1 hour in the cold water and white vinegar.
— Drain and clean carefully, making sure to remove the membranes, small red veins and black spots.
— Place the brains in a dish and add the bay leaves, garlic, salt, pepper and hot water.
— Cover and cook for 5 to 8 minutes at 100%.
— Let the brains stand for 2 minutes, remove from the cooking liquid and set aside.
— Preheat a browning dish for 4 minutes at 100% and add the butter and parsley. Cook the butter until brown.
— Pour the brown butter over the brains and serve immediately.

* The brains must be soaked for at least 2 hours in cold water before cooking.

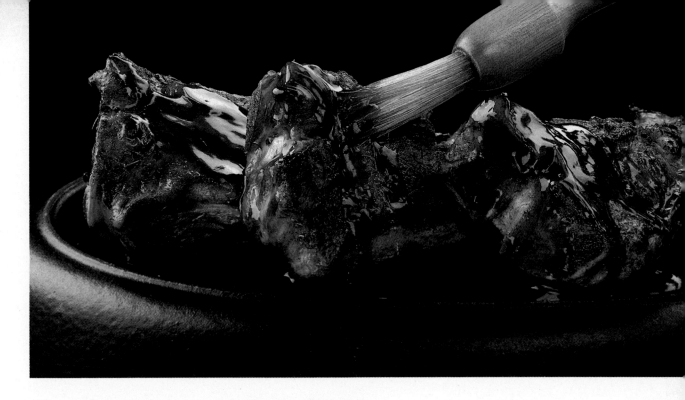

Lamb Chops Italian Style

Level of Difficulty	🍴
Preparation Time	10 min*
Cost per Serving	$ $
Number of Servings	2
Nutritional Value	297 calories 19.6 g protein 2.2 mg iron
Food Exchanges	3 oz meat 1-1/2 fat exchanges
Cooking Time	9 min
Standing Time	None
Power Level	100%, 70%
Write Your Cooking Time Here	

* The meat must be marinated for 6 to 8 hours before cooking.

Ingredients
4 lamb chops
45 mL (3 tablespoons) water
30 mL (2 tablespoons) lemon juice
75 mL (1/3 cup) oil
4 cloves garlic, cut in half
5 mL (1 teaspoon) pepper
5 mL (1 teaspoon) oregano

Method
— First prepare the marinade by mixing all the ingredients other than the lamb chops in a dish.
— Place the chops in the marinade, cover and leave to marinate for 6 to 8 hours in the refrigerator.
— Preheat a browning dish for 7 minutes at 100%, dry the chops well and sear them.
— Reduce the power level to 70% and cook uncovered for 6 to 9 minutes, or until the chops are done to your liking.

Cuts of Lamb

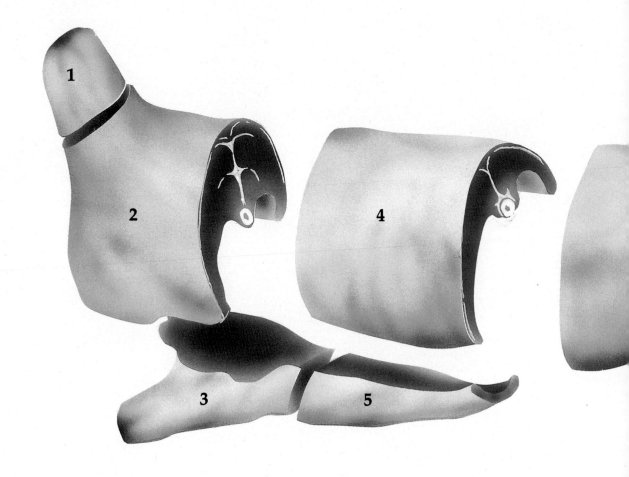

1. The Neck. An inexpensive cut but tasty and tender, the neck is sold whole or cut into slices. It may be braised or used to make lamb stock and soups.

2. The Shoulder. Blade chops, arm chops and shoulder roasts are cut from the shoulder. A boned and rolled lamb shoulder makes a very tender roast. The shoulder can also be cut into cubes for kebabs or stewing meat.

3. The Foreshank. The meat from the front legs of the lamb may be braised whole or used in simmered casseroles.

4. The Rack or Rib. This section makes an excellent rib roast (rack of lamb), which may or may not be arranged in a crown shape. It may also be cut into rib chops.

5. The Breast. This is a less choice cut which is quite fatty but tasty. It contains bones also and provides side ribs. It can be purchased boned and rolled and it may be stuffed and roasted or braised.

6. The Loin. A choice cut containing between 12 and 14 ribs, the loin can be sold whole and dry roasted. It may be boned and rolled—it is

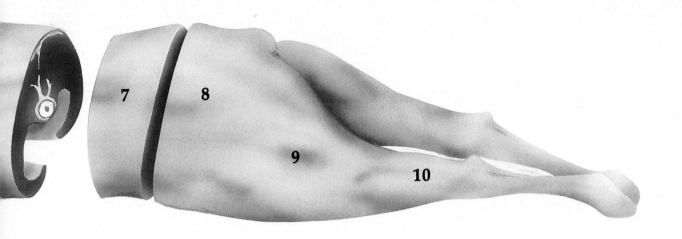

then called a rolled double loin, or saddle, roast. The loin may also be cut into loin chops or double boneless loin chops, which are broiled, grilled or pan fried.

7. The Sirloin. This can be cut into sirloin chops or served whole, as a sirloin roast. It may also be boned and rolled.

8. The Leg, Butt End. This, upper, part of the leg is the meatiest and the tastiest. It provides leg chops, or steaks, as well as what is known as leg of lamb, center cut.

9 and 10. The Leg, Shank End. Sold whole or cut into two, the upper part (9), which is often boned and rolled, makes a more meaty roast, while the lower part (10), the hind shank, contains less meat and is usually braised. The hind shank is also sometimes cut into cubes for stewing or ground to make lamb patties.

Buying and Storing Lamb

Buying Lamb

As with veal, lamb dishes start with a well-chosen piece of meat. Not only is this the first step, but probably the most important because all of the meat's inherent characteristics will have a considerable impact on the flavor and, consequently, on the dish you serve.

Meat sold under the name of lamb does not necessarily come from a very young animal. Young mutton, that is, lamb over one year old, may be sold as lamb without this being considered as a misrepresentation. Age is not the only factor in determining what is lamb and what is mutton. The dividing line may change according to the region and the type of rearing. In any case, whether it is lamb or mutton, the meat will be tender if it is fresh. The age of the animal, however, will have a great influence on the flavor—the older the animal, the stronger the taste.

Fortunately, it is possible to get a fairly good idea of the animal's age by examining the meat very carefully. The flesh of a young lamb is more pink than red. The fat is smooth and pinkish white. The bones are porous and pale pink and the flesh and fat are firm to the touch. (If the flesh and fat are not firm, this does not necessarily mean that the lamb is older, rather that the meat is no longer fresh.)

The flesh of one-year-old lamb and young mutton is brighter red than that of a young lamb. The bones are very white and so is the fat—the latter almost looks like wax. The fat and flesh must be very firm. If you do not care for the stronger taste of the older animal, avoid buying lamb with a relatively rough texture.

When buying a whole leg of lamb, you can use the weight as an indication of the quality of the meat and the age of the animal. A leg weighing 2 to 2-1/2 kg (4 to 5-1/2 lb) comes from a young lamb. It will have a delicate taste and tender flesh. If it weighs 3-1/2 to 4 kg (7 to 9 lb), it is probably from a young sheep and will have a stronger flavor and more fat. It may also be a bit less tender.

Lamb that is not fresh has fat that is somewhat yellow in color and oily flesh. Frozen lamb will give you better results than lamb that is not fresh.

Although breeding is no longer left to nature and lambing can now take place all year round, lamb remains a seasonal meat, as evidenced by the fact that more fresh lamb is put on the market in the spring. Locally raised lamb is at its best in the spring and early summer—which is also when it is the least expensive. During the rest of the year fresh "spring" lamb is extremely expensive; it is therefore more economical to buy frozen New Zealand lamb then.

Storing Lamb

Lamb is a meat that does not pose any particular storage problems. Its taste is not easily destroyed and its flesh contains enough fat to protect it from drying out. It retains all its qualities in the refrigerator and is also suitable for freezing. This does not mean, however, that you can refrigerate or freeze it in a careless way. Like any other meat, its storage time is limited; it will become rancid if kept in the refrigerator too long and will dry out if kept in the freezer too long. Moreover, it will be severely damaged if the package or container is not suitable.

Although we have said it before, the fact that it is essential to refrigerate the meat as soon as possible after buying it bears repeating. If you leave it until it reaches room temperature, not only will bacteria multiply but its potential storage time will be reduced.

Also, be careful to protect the meat from the cold, dry air circulating in the refrigerator, which can dry it out and alter its flavor. Meat that is improperly packaged is not only damaged by the air but it puts the other food in the refrigerator at risk as well; the oxygen causes the juice and fat to go rancid and this taste will permeate the other food. Carefully examine the packaging of the meat you buy before refrigerating it. If the package is not tightly sealed, change it immediately, first wrapping it tightly in plastic wrap. Do the same if the meat package is torn, even slightly. Never buy a package of meat that has been damaged.

Lamb is particularly well suited to freezing—all you have to do is look at the enormous quantities of frozen lamb available commercially. We might note that the meat is frozen in optimal industrial conditions and that vacuum-sealed packages, which are airtight, watertight and very sturdy, are used. If you want to freeze lamb yourself, try coming as close as possible to the techniques used commercially. Avoid using the packages in which the meat was purchased because they are too fragile. If you can't vacuum-seal the meat for freezing, then at least wrap it in strong, airtight and watertight packages, removing as much air as possible. Put a label on the package showing the date on which it was frozen and the maximum time that it can be safely stored.

Consult the chart below as a guide to length of time that different cuts of lamb may be safely stored in the refrigerator and in the freezer.

Storage Times for Lamb

Cut	Refrigerator	Freezer*
Roasts	3 to 5 days	6 to 8 months
Loin and rib chops	3 to 4 days	4 to 6 months
Side ribs	2 days	3 to 4 months
Stuffed lamb	24 hours	3 to 4 months
Cubes	2 days	3 to 4 months
Ground lamb	24 days	3 to 4 months
Offal (heart, liver, etc.)	1 to 2 days	3 months
Cooked lamb	7 days	3 months

* Lamb kept in the freezer must be put into airtight and watertight packages; otherwise, the cold, dry air may cause freezer burn.

Defrosting Lamb

Defrosting could actually be considered a final stage in the storage of meat; proper defrosting methods are therefore just as vital as proper freezing. If it is not done correctly, all the precautions taken to keep the meat fresh will be to no avail —improper treatment at this stage has the same degree of influence on the flavor and texture as would improper freezing techniques.

For lamb, as for other meats, the best defrosting method is unfortunately the slowest one: removing the meat from the freezer and putting it in the refrigerator until it is evenly thawed. Our schedules, however, do not always allow us to do this—which is where the microwave comes in handy. Without too much trouble, you can use it to defrost cuts as large as legs of lamb quickly and evenly.

To have control over the results, however, you must obviously keep a few basic rules in mind.

Defrosting Chops and Equivalent Cuts

Rib chops, loin chops and other flat cuts are usually irregular in shape and have bony parts that must be taken into account when defrosting. Always put them on a bacon rack or an upside-down plate inside another dish.

The idea here is to avoid having the meat come into contact with the juices that seep out during defrosting. As we know, microwaves heat liquids very quickly and these liquids could start to cook the meat before it is completely defrosted.

Ideally, you should take the meat out of the package and separate the pieces before putting them on the rack. This will be easy if you took the trouble to insert one or two layers of plastic wrap between the pieces before you froze them.

If the pieces have been frozen together and it is impossible to take them out of the package, put the package in the oven for a short defrosting period and then take them out of the package and separate them.

Arrange the pieces so that the bony and less meaty parts are toward the center, where they are the least exposed to the microwaves. Divide the total defrosting time into two periods. During the first period, when the meat is half defrosted turn the pieces, leaving the bony parts in the center. Cover any defrosted parts with aluminum foil before beginning the second period.

At the end of the second period let the meat stand for five minutes, allowing the internal temperature to be evenly distributed. If you can pierce the meat with a fork at this point, it is completely defrosted.

Defrosting Cubes

Since cubes of lamb are normally frozen in packages or in a container, leave them packaged when you first put them into the microwave. Divide the total defrosting time into two periods. After the first period, remove the cubes from the package, separate them, place them on a dish and put them back for a second defrosting period. At the end of this cycle, their surface should be soft. Let them stand for 5 to 10 minutes to allow the internal temperature to be evenly distributed. If you can pierce them with a fork, they are completely defrosted.

Defrosting Roasts

In defrosting large cuts, such as leg of lamb, you must take care not to allow certain parts to start to cook before others are completely defrosted. If you take no precautions, the small end of the leg as well as any parts that are in contact with the bottom of the dish will become very hot and will begin to cook while the center is still frozen.

You must also ensure that the meat loses as little juice as possible to prevent flavor loss. For best results, follow these steps:

1. To prevent the meat from coming into contact with its juice, put a meat rack or upside-down saucer in a dish and stand the meat on it. This is especially important because the microwaves are attracted to liquids and heat them quickly. Any part of the meat that is in contact with the juice will therefore start to cook before the center of the meat is defrosted.

2. Before defrosting, cover the last 5 cm (2 in) of the end of the leg with aluminum foil. Since it has little meat on it, this part defrosts quickly and premature cooking can be avoided with this technique.

3. At the end of the first defrosting period, feel the meat and cover any defrosted parts with aluminum foil (the ends, in particular). In this way, the microwaves will have an equal effect over the whole cut.

4. Divide the total defrosting time into several short periods, with standing times, equivalent in total to one quarter of the total defrosting time, in between the defrosting cycles.

Consult the chart below for recommended defrosting times for different cuts of lamb.

Defrosting Guide*

Cut	Defrosting Time at 50%	Defrosting Time at 25%
Roasts	17 to 22 min/kg (8 to 10 min/lb)	22 to 26 min/kg (10 to 12 min/lb)
Legs	17 to 22 min/kg (8 to 10 min/lb)	22 to 26 min/kg (10 to 12 min/lb)
Loin and rib chops	6 to 14 min/kg (3 to 6 min/lb)	8 to 17 min/kg (4 to 8 min/lb)
Cubes	6 to 10 min/kg (3 to 5 min/lb)	8 to 14 min/kg (4 to 6 min/lb)
Ground lamb	6 to 10 min/kg (3 to 5 min/lb)	10 to 17 min/kg (5 to 8 min/lb)

* Don't forget to divide the defrosting time given into two or three periods in the microwave with periods of standing time, which are equal in total to a quarter of the total amount of the defrosting time, between the defrosting cycles.

Cooking Lamb

Given that lamb is relatively expensive, it is understandable that some people hesitate to try cooking it for the first time in a microwave oven. As food cooks so quickly in the microwave, they are apprehensive about ending up with a leg of lamb that is too well done or chops that are completely dried out.

They needn't worry, however; lamb is really quite easy to prepare and cook—it is certainly no more complicated than beef. Cooking times are related to the cut of meat, its weight and the power level at which it is cooked. The temperature of the meat when it is put into the oven is also important, as is water, fat and bone content. These factors are all taken into account in the cooking times given in the chart on page 67, opposite. If you follow them, you will have a dish that will please even the most difficult guest.

Characteristics of Lamb

Except for milk-fed lamb, which is exceptionally tender and lean, lamb is comparable to beef. It is a red meat, fairly well marbled and has about the same degree of tenderness. It is best served somewhere between rare and medium. When well done, it tends to be tough and its flavor deteriorates. This change in flavor is due to the fact that the fat, especially that of older lambs, has a strong, tallowy taste that can easily permeate the flesh.

This latter point, however, does not mean you have to stick to milk-fed lamb, which is only seasonally available, rare and expensive. Cuts from older animals—young sheep, for example—can be excellent if you remember to trim the fat before cooking them. The older the lamb or young sheep, the more carefully the fat must be trimmed. (Note that a sweet-and-sour sauce with vinegar base can be used to mask any unpleasant taste from the fat if the animal is older.)

Many recipes call for marinating lamb before cooking it. The flavor of the marinade will penetrate best if the meat is fresh and marinated as soon as you buy it. To cook small cuts evenly, be careful about the way in which they are arranged in the microwave—bony parts toward the center of the dish.

Cooking a leg of lamb is a different matter; it is large, has an irregular shape and must be cooked slowly. The microwaves have the same effect on the end of the leg, which is less meaty, as they will have on the fattier parts which attract the microwaves or the center which is less exposed. To cook evenly, shield the end by covering the last 5 cm (2 inches) with aluminum foil. When placing the leg in a dish, put the fattiest part on the bottom and, halfway through the cooking time, turn the meat over.

Consult the chart to the right for guidelines as to recommended cooking times for lamb.

Cooking Times for Lamb

Cut	Power Level	Cooking Time
Loin and rib chops	70%	19 to 24 min/kg (9 to 11 min/lb)
Cubes, braised	50%	50 to 66 min/kg (23 to 30 min/lb)
Leg		
Rare	70%	28 min/kg (13 min/lb)
Medium	70%	33 min/kg (15 min/lb)
Well done	70%	37 min/kg (17 min/lb)
Rolled shoulder roasts		
Rare	70%	28 min/kg (13 min/lb)
Medium	70%	33 min/kg (15 min/lb)
Well done	70%	37 min/kg (17 min/lb)
Ground lamb	70%	9 to 14 min/kg (4-1/2 to 6 min/lb)

MICROTIPS

To Defrost Half a Package of Vegetables

When you need only half a package of frozen vegetables, you can use the microwave to defrost it without affecting the other half.

Wrap half the package in aluminum foil and put the entire package in the microwave for a first defrosting period. Remove the half you want to use, take off the aluminum foil, close the package and return it to the freezer. Finish defrosting the partially defrosted half in a container.

Arranging Cuts of Lamb in the Oven

To obtain pleasing results when cooking lamb in the microwave, you must make sure it cooks evenly. Roasts, ribs, chops and cubes must be correctly arranged in the oven and moved around in different ways, depending on the cuts. By following a few simple rules, you can avoid disappointment.

Leg of Lamb

Leg of lamb can be cooked in an open dish, without broth, or covered and braised in liquid. Cooking it in a covered dish does not pose any particular problem—you simply carefully remove the largest pieces of fat before putting it in the oven and baste it periodically during cooking.

Cooking in an open dish, on the other hand, requires certain precautions. First, you must make sure the underside of the leg does not remain in the juice that escapes from the meat. Put the leg on a meat rack, which you then place in a dish. The leg will cook more evenly if you place the fattiest part on the rack. If you are cooking a large leg, from an older animal, carefully remove the fat before cooking so that the taste of the fat does not permeate the meat. Cover the last 5 cm (2 in) of the end with aluminum foil as this part, being less meaty, tends to cook faster. Finally, turn the leg over halfway through the cooking time.

Lamb Kebabs

Cubes are most often used for kebabs, which are always popular. To cook them correctly, place wooden skewers over the ends of a dish so that the cubes are suspended. Halfway through the cooking time, move the skewers that were in the center to the outside of the dish and vice-versa.

Loin and Rib Chops

These are usually cooked on a meat rack placed inside a dish. Always place the less meaty and bony parts in the center of the dish where the microwaves are less intense. The meat near the bone tends to cook more quickly and, as the microwaves are more powerful around the outside of the dish, arranging the chops in the manner described brings about a balance in these two contrary effects and the meat will cook more evenly. As well, it is important to divide the total cooking time into two periods and to turn the chops over when they are half cooked, always being careful to keep the bony parts in the center of the dish.

Testing Lamb for Doneness

Leg of lamb is a red meat and is comparable to beef as far as its tenderness and method of cooking are concerned. If it is cooked for too long, however, it quickly loses its tenderness and flavor. It should therefore be served rare or medium, never well done.

Meat thermometers are efficient tools for checking the degree to which meat is done. When the cooking time is over, remove the leg of lamb from the oven and insert the thermometer to within 2-1/2 cm (1 in) from the bone. If the internal temperature has reached 63°C (145°F), the roast will be rare. If it has reached 68°C (155°F), it will be medium. In both cases, cover the leg with aluminum foil and let it stand for 10 minutes so that the heat becomes evenly distributed. The internal temperature will rise a few more degrees.

A second method for checking the meat involves carving a slice off the roast and checking color. The leg is rare if there is a thin band of brown around the edge and the remainder is still pink to red. It is medium if almost half the meat is brown and the center is still pink. When the lamb has reached the desired degree of doneness, cover it with aluminum foil and let it stand for 10 minutes.

Lamb Chops with Orange Sauce

Level of Difficulty	
Preparation Time	10 min
Cost per Serving	$ $
Number of Servings	4
Nutritional Value	548 calories 33.5 g protein 3.8 mg iron
Food Exchanges	4 oz meat 1-1/2 fat exchanges 3 fruit exchanges
Cooking Time	12 min
Standing Time	5 min
Power Level	100%, 70%
Write Your Cooking Time Here	

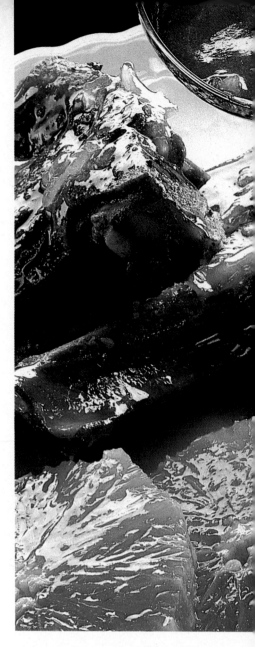

Ingredients
8 lamb shoulder chops
250 mL (1 cup) orange marmalade
30 mL (2 tablespoons) butter
15 mL (1 tablespoon) dry sherry
1 clove garlic, chopped
5 mL (1 teaspoon) salt

Method
— Combine all the ingredients, except the lamb, in a dish and mix well.
— Cook at 100% for 2 to 3 minutes, or until the mixture has melted, stirring each minutes.
— Add the lamb chops, making sure to cover with the sauce.
— Reduce the power level to 70% and cook for 7 to 9 minutes, or until the meat is done to your liking, giving the dish a half-turn every 3 minutes.
— Let stand for 5 minutes before serving.

MICROTIPS

Choosing Lamb

To choose a cut of lamb that is suitable for the dish you are making, you must know the characteristics of this type of meat. First, lamb is not classified into categories that are as distinct as those for beef and veal. Canada has no real standardized classification system for it. Nevertheless, the system that does exist takes into account the quality of the muscle structure, age of the animal and amount of fat.

The grades go from A1 to A4. A1 has the leanest meat and comes from the youngest lambs. A4 comes from young sheep, which contain more fat. This grading system is intended for local production only, however imported lamb is frozen and marketed without being graded. Meat from young sheep takes up the greatest share of the market. Baby (or milk-fed) lamb is very tender but also very rare and has a rather bland flavor. It is mainly found in specialized butcher shops.

Crown Roast of Lamb with Apricots

Level of Difficulty	🍴
Preparation Time	20 min
Cost per Serving	$ $ $
Number of Servings	4
Nutritional Value	563 calories 37.3 g protein 6.2 mg iron
Food Exchanges	4 oz meat 1-1/2 fat exchanges 1-1/2 fruit exchanges 1-1/2 bread exchanges
Cooking Time	1 h 50 min
Standing Time	10 min
Power Level	100%, 50%
Write Your Cooking Time Here	

Ingredients
2 racks of lamb, tied together to form a crown
125 mL (1/2 cup) hot chicken broth
chives, chopped

Stuffing:
50 mL (1/4 cup) butter
2 onions, chopped
4 stalks celery, chopped
6 slices of bread, crusts removed
250 mL (1 cup) apricots, peeled and chopped
12 prunes, soaked and pitted, cut in half
salt and pepper to taste
pinch fine herbs

Method
— To make the stuffing, first melt the butter in a dish at 100% for 1 minute.
— Add the onions and celery; cover and cook for 3 to 4 minutes at 100%.
— Add the bread, apricots, prunes and seasonings; mix well and set aside.
— Place the lamb in a dish and cover the ends of the ribs with aluminum foil.
— Pour the hot chicken broth over it and sprinkle with chives.
— Cover and cook for 1 hour at 50%, giving the dish a half-turn after 30 minutes.
— Fill the crown with the stuffing and remove the foil.
— Cover and cook at 50% for 30 to 45 minutes, or until the meat is tender, giving the dish a half-turn after 20 minutes.
— Let stand for 10 minutes before serving.

MICROTIPS

To Dry Fine Herbs

When you buy fresh herbs, or if you grow them yourself, you may find you have too many to use right away. But with a microwave oven you can dry them quickly and save them for later use.

1. Arrange the fresh herbs in a circle on a paper towel in the microwave.

2. Set the oven at 100% and turn the herbs over every 30 seconds.

3. Stop as soon as the leaves break when you touch them (probably after 1 to 2 minutes). Let stand for 12 hours, crumble and put in sealed containers.

To Remove the Fat from Ground Meat

Those who want to reduce their intake of animal fat will appreciate this simple tip for removing fat from ground meat: place the meat in a plastic strainer, put it in the oven over a container to catch the melted fat; cook the meat and then add it to the dish you are making.

Note: The strainer should not have any metal parts.

Leg of Lamb with Rosemary

Level of Difficulty	🍴
Preparation Time	10 min*
Cost per Serving	$ $ $
Number of Servings	10
Nutritional Value	258 calories 38.4 g protein 2.7 mg iron
Food Exchanges	4-1/2 oz meat
Cooking Time	33 min/kg (15 min/lb)
Standing Time	10 min
Power Level	70%
Write Your Cooking Time Here	

* The lamb should be left to marinate at room temperature for at least 1 hour before cooking.

Ingredients
1 1.8 kg (4 lb) leg of lamb
5 mL (1 teaspoon) pepper
5 mL (1 teaspoon) ginger
10 mL (2 teaspoons) rosemary
15 mL (1 tablespoon) oil
50 mL (1/4 cup) breadcrumbs

Method
— Combine the pepper, ginger, rosemary and oil to make the paste.
— Brush the leg of lamb with the paste and allow to marinate for 1 hour at room temperature.
— Place on a rack in a dish.
— If the leg of lamb is irregular in shape, cover the thinner parts with aluminum foil to avoid overcooking.
— Sprinkle with breadcrumbs and cook uncovered at 70%, allowing 33 min/kg (15 min/lb) if you want it cooked medium. Give the dish a half-turn and baste with the cooking juices halfway through the cooking time.

Leg of Lamb Glazed with Cranberries

Level of Difficulty	
Preparation Time	10 min
Cost per Serving	$ $ $
Number of Servings	10
Nutritional Value	258 calories 38.2 g protein 2.7 mg iron
Food Exchanges	4-1/2 oz meat
Cooking Time	33 min/kg (15 min/lb) + 3 min
Standing Time	10 min
Power Level	70%, 100%
Write Your Cooking Time Here	

Ingredients
1 leg of lamb
15 mL (1 tablespoon) oregano
175 mL (3/4 cup) cranberries
15 mL (1 tablespoon) orange zest
15 mL (1 tablespoon) lemon juice

Method
— Sprinkle the lamb with the oregano and place on a meat rack in a dish.
— For medium lamb, cook at 70% for 33 min/kg (15 min/lb); halfway through the cooking time, give the dish a half-turn and cover the parts that are cooked with foil.
— While the lamb is cooking combine the remaining ingredients; 10 minutes before the cooking time is up, remove the leg, cook the cranberry mixture at 100% for 2 to 3 minutes, stirring once, and then glaze the lamb with it.
— Continue to cook the lamb at 70%, basting with the glaze every 4 minutes.
— Let stand for 10 minutes before serving.

Sprinkle the leg of lamb with oregano to give it a distinctive flavor.

Set the lamb on a meat rack and then place the rack in a dish.

Halfway through the cooking time, cover those parts that are cooked with aluminum foil.

MICROTIPS

For Tender Lamb

A large piece of meat such as a leg of lamb is usually seasoned before cooking for the best flavor. Salt, however, should not be added until the end because it tends to toughen the meat.

Lamb Chops with Apples

Level of Difficulty	♨
Preparation Time	20 min
Cost per Serving	$ $
Number of Servings	4
Nutritional Value	474 calories 26.6 g protein 4.3 mg iron
Food Exchanges	4 oz meat 2 fat exchanges 1 fruit exchange 1 bread exchange
Cooking Time	19 min
Standing Time	10 min
Power Level	100%, 70%
Write Your Cooking Time Here	

Ingredients
8 lamb chops
6 red potatoes, sliced
4 onions, sliced
50 mL (1/4 cup) water
45 mL (3 tablespoons) butter
125 mL (1/2 cup) chicken broth
125 mL (1/2 cup) apple juice
4 apples, sliced
50 mL (1/4 cup) Parmesan cheese, grated

Method
— Place the potatoes and onions in a dish; add the water, cover and cook at 100% for 4 to 5 minutes, stirring once.
— Drain the liquid and set the cooked vegetables aside.
— Preheat a browning dish for 7 minutes at 100%; add the butter and heat for 30 seconds at 100%.
— Sear the chops, remove and set aside.
— Use the chicken broth to deglaze the dish and heat for 1 minute at 100%; scrape the bottom with a spatula; add the apple juice and cook for 2 minutes at 100% and set the liquid aside.
— Place half the potato and onion mixture in another dish and arrange the lamb chops on top.
— Put the remaining vegetable mixture on top and cover with the apple slices.
— Add the reserved liquid to the assembled dish and reduce the power level to 70%; cover and cook for 9 to 11 minutes, giving the dish a half-turn after 5 minutes.
— Sprinkle with the Parmesan, cover once more and let stand for 10 minutes before serving.

Place half the cooked vegetables in a dish and set the lamb chops on top of them. Cover with the remaining vegetables and then top with apple slices. Pour the reserved liquid over the assembled dish.

When the chops are done, sprinkle with the Parmesan cheese, cover and let stand for 10 minutes.

Shank of Lamb European Style

Level of Difficulty	🍴
Preparation Time	15 min
Cost per Serving	$
Number of Servings	4
Nutritional Value	251 calories 25.5 g protein 3 mg iron
Food Exchanges	3 oz meat 1-1/2 fat exchanges 1 vegetable exchange
Cooking Time	29 min
Standing Time	5 min
Power Level	100%, 70%
Write Your Cooking Time Here	

Ingredients
4 pieces of lamb shank, weighing 225 g (8 oz) each
30 mL (2 tablespoons) butter
1 onion, sliced
4 carrots, cut into sticks
2 stalks celery, cut into sticks
30 mL (2 tablespoons) flour
1 398 mL (14 oz) can tomato sauce
5 mL (1 teaspoon) salt
1 clove garlic, chopped
1 bay leaf
2 mL (1/2 teaspoon) thyme

Method
— Preheat a browning dish for 7 minutes at 100%; add the butter and heat for 30 seconds at 100%.
— Sear the onion, carrots and celery; sprinkle with the flour and mix well.
— Add all the other ingredients, except the lamb, and cook at 100% for 3 to 4 minutes or until the mixture is hot, stirring every 2 minutes.
— Add the pieces of lamb shank, cover, reduce the power level to 70% and cook for 20 to 25 minutes, or until the meat comes away from the bone, giving the dish a half-turn and turning the lamb over once during the cooking time.
— Let stand for 5 minutes before serving.

Most people don't realize how tasty lamb shanks really are. Here are the ingredients you will need to make this European-style dish.

Sear the vegetables in butter in the preheated browning dish.

When all the other ingredients are hot, add the pieces of shank and cook as directed.

Lamb Stew

Ingredients
6 lamb chops
30 mL (2 tablespoons) oil
2 stalks celery, sliced
4 carrots, sliced

2 onions, chopped
250 mL (1 cup) water
150 mL (2/3 cup) dry
vermouth
pinch marjoram

pinch thyme
pinch cumin
salt and pepper to taste
15 mL (1 tablespoon) vinegar
15 mL (1 tablespoon) honey
5 mL (1 tablespoon) Dijon
mustard

Level of Difficulty	🍴🍴
Preparation Time	20 min
Cost per Serving	$ $
Number of Servings	2
Nutritional Value	486 calories 33.4 g protein 4.8 mg iron
Food Exchanges	4-1/2 oz meat 3 vegetable exchanges 2 fat exchanges
Cooking Time	20 min
Standing Time	10 min
Power Level	100%, 70%
Write Your Cooking Time Here	

Method
— Preheat a browning dish at 100% for 7 minutes; add the oil and heat at 100% for 30 seconds.
— Sear the lamb chops and then add all the other ingredients.
— Reduce the power level to 70%; cover and cook for 15 to 20 minutes, giving the dish a half-turn after 8 minutes.
— Let stand for 10 minutes before serving.

Braised Lamb Chops with Vegetables

Ingredients
900 g (2 lb) lamb, cut into
2.5 cm (1 in) cubes

50 mL (1/4 cup) oil
2 onions, sliced
1 red pepper, cut into thin

strips
1 stalk celery, finely sliced
500 mL (2 cups) beef broth
15 mL (1 tablespoon) tomato
paste
salt and pepper to taste

Level of Difficulty	🍴
Preparation Time	20 min
Cost per Serving	$
Number of Servings	6
Nutritional Value	312 calories 34.4 g protein 2.8 mg iron
Food Exchanges	4 oz meat 1 vegetable exchange 1-1/2 fat exchanges
Cooking Time	1 h 14 min
Standing Time	10 min
Power Level	100%, 50%
Write Your Cooking Time Here	✏️🍎

Method
— In a dish, combine the oil, onions, red pepper strips and celery; cover and cook at 100% for 3 to 4 minutes, stirring after 2 minutes.
— Add the lamb cubes, the beef broth and tomato paste, and season.
— Reduce the power level to 50%; cover and cook for 30 minutes.
— Stir, cover once more and continue to cook at 50% for 30 to 40 minutes, or until the meat is tender.
— Let stand for 10 minutes before serving.

Roast Lamb with Madeira

Level of Difficulty	🍴
Preparation Time	5 min
Cost per Serving	$ $ $
Number of Servings	10
Nutritional Value	292 calories 38.2 g protein 2.7 mg iron
Food Exchanges	4 oz meat 1/2 fat exchange
Cooking Time	33 min/kg (15 min/lb) + 1 min
Standing Time	10 min
Power Level	100%, 70%
Write Your Cooking Time Here	

Ingredients
1 1.8 kg (4 lb) roast of lamb
50 mL (1/4 cup) Madeira
15 mL (1 tablespoon) paprika
30 mL (2 tablespoons) oil
2 cloves garlic, chopped

Method
— In a dish, mix the Madeira, paprika, oil and garlic.
— Heat for 60 to 90 seconds at 100%.
— Place the roast on a rack in a dish and brush with the hot mixture.
— Reduce the power level to 70% and cook uncovered for 33 min/kg (15 min/lb). Give the dish a half-turn and baste the roast with its cooking juices halfway through the cooking time.
— Let stand for 10 minutes before carving.

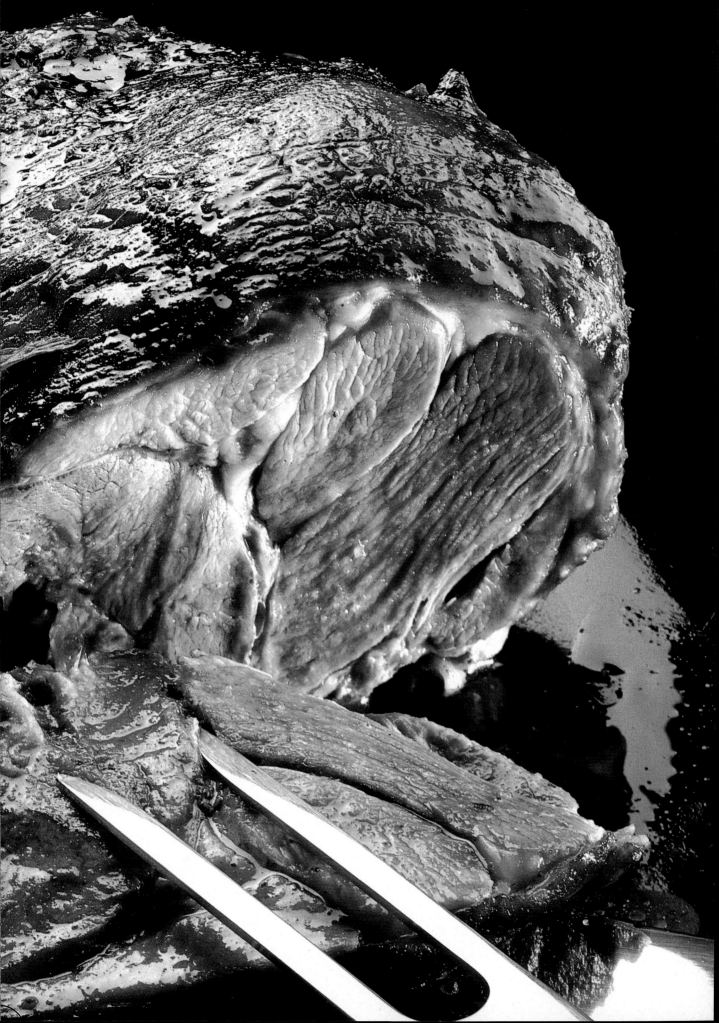

Glazed Lamb Shoulder

Level of Difficulty	🍴
Preparation Time	10 min
Cost per Serving	$ $ $
Number of Servings	10
Nutritional Value	326 calories 35.7 g protein 2.3 mg iron
Food Exchanges	4 oz meat 1 fruit exchange
Cooking Time	33 min/kg (15 min/lb) + 1 min
Standing Time	10 min
Power Level	70%, 100%
Write Your Cooking Time Here	✏️🍎

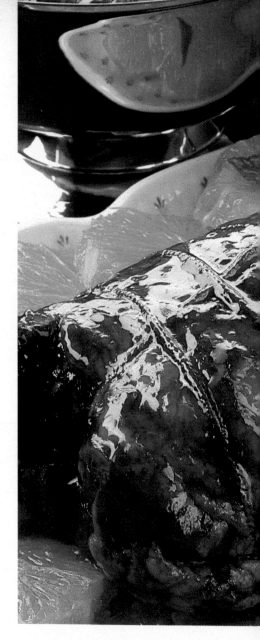

Ingredients
1 1.3 to 1.8 kg (3 to 4 lb) lamb shoulder roast
125 mL (1/2 cup) marmalade
5 mL (1 teaspoon) salt
2 mL (1/2 teaspoon) pepper
30 mL (2 tablespoons) flour
30 mL (2 tablespoons) parsley, chopped

Method
— Place the shoulder of lamb on a meat rack so that the side with the fat is on the bottom.
— In a bowl, combine the marmalade, salt and pepper; mix well and set aside.
— Cook the meat uncovered at 70% for 33 min/kg (15 min/lb).
— Halfway through the cooking time, turn the meat over so that the fat side is up. Sprinkle flour over the surface and brush with the prepared glaze; continue to cook, basting periodically with the glaze.
— When done, remove the meat and let stand for 10 minutes; baste once more and then place on a serving platter.
— Stir the glaze remaining in the bottom of the rack, increase the power level to 100% and heat for 45 to 60 seconds.
— Pour the hot glaze over the meat and sprinkle with parsley before carving.

Place the lamb shoulder on a meat rack, making sure that the side with the fat is on the bottom.

Halfway through the cooking time, turn the meat over so that the fat side is up.

Brush the meat with the prepared glaze.

Rack of Lamb French Style

Level of Difficulty	🍴🍴 🍴🍴 🍴🍴
Preparation Time	30 min
Cost per Serving	$ $ $
Number of Servings	4
Nutritional Value	266 calories 39.2 g protein 4.4 mg iron
Food Exchanges	4 oz meat
Cooking Time	57 min
Standing Time	10 min
Power Level	50%, 100%
Write Your Cooking Time Here	

Ingredients
2 racks of lamb, 8 ribs each and "Frenched" (rib tips stripped of meat; see photograph)
pepper to taste
5 mL (1 teaspoon) aniseed
2 cloves garlic, crushed
30 mL (2 tablespoons) wine vinegar
7 mL (1/2 tablespoon) sugar
salt and pepper to taste

Method
— Join the two racks so their concave sides face one another.
— Link the ribs of each rack through those of the other, as shown in the accompanying photograph.
— In three different places, tie the racks together vertically so that the ribs are intertwined.
— Place the racks in a dish.
— Cover the scraped rib ends with aluminum foil, sprinkle the meat with pepper and aniseed and rub some of the garlic into the surface of the meat.
— Cover and cook at 50% for 35 minutes for rare meat or for 55 minutes for medium.
— Let stand for 10 minutes and remove the racks from the dish.
— Put the remaining garlic in the bottom of the dish, add the wine vinegar and sugar and cook at 100% for 1 to 2 minutes, stirring twice during the cooking time.
— Season to taste, spoon the liquid over the lamb and serve.

MICROTIPS

Two Traditional Sauces for Lamb

Lamb is a tender meat with a distinctive flavor. It is therefore best to enhance it with sauces that are quite strong. Here are two traditional sauces that are always enjoyed with lamb.

Mint sauce is customarily served by the English. Its sharp taste is very good for masking the strong flavor that fattier pieces of lamb sometimes take on. It is made by combining fresh mint leaves with a little boiling water and granulated sugar and marinating them together. Vinegar is added just before serving.

Pesto sauce offers quite another taste experience. You make the traditional French *pistou* by mashing cloves of garlic and fresh basil leaves together, seasoning with salt and pepper and adding olive oil to make a paste. Some pesto recipes recommend adding grated Parmesan cheese and peeled tomatoes that have been chopped and seeded. Pesto can be rubbed into lamb or added to sauces made for it to make a "pesto" sauce.

Lamb Kebabs

Level of Difficulty	🍴
Preparation Time	15 min
Cost per Serving	$ $ $
Number of Servings	6
Nutritional Value	347 calories 47.6 g protein 7.7 mg iron
Food Exchanges	5 oz meat 1 vegetable exchange
Cooking Time	12 min
Standing Time	None
Power Level	90%, 70%
Write Your Cooking Time Here	

Ingredients
675 g (1-1/2 lb) baby lamb
shoulder or leg
2 lamb kidneys, trimmed
225 g (8 oz) mushrooms,
stems removed
8 cherry tomatoes
1 green pepper, cut into
chunks
1 zucchini, sliced across
30 mL (2 tablespoons) oil
15 mL (1 tablespoon) lemon
juice
30 mL (2 tablespoons)
parsley, chopped

Method
— Cut the meat into 2.5 cm
(1 in) cubes and cut the
kidneys into four pieces.
— Skewer the vegetables and
lamb cubes and kidneys
alternately on wooden
skewers, making sure that
the cherry tomatoes are
placed in the center.
Combine the oil, lemon
juice and parsley in a bowl
and brush the skewered
pieces with the mixture.
— Set the skewers on a dish
with their ends over the
edges so that the skewered
pieces are suspended.

— Cover the dish and cook
for 4 minutes at 90%.
— Brush the skewered pieces
once again, rearranging
their positions on the dish
to ensure even cooking
and cover once more.
— Reduce the power level to
70% and continue to cook
for 4 to 8 minutes, or until
the lamb is done to your
liking.

MICROTIPS

To Make the Most of Dried Herbs

Dried herbs lose their seasoning power quite quickly. To get the most out of them, buy them in small quantities and renew your supply frequently. Keep them, in small sealed containers, but don't fill the containers completely because a certain amount of air is necessary for preserving dried herbs.

To Keep Parsley and Watercress Fresh

Parsley and watercress are often sold in quantities too large to be used all at once. You can keep them fresh for several days, however, by washing and drying them well, putting them in a jar with a screw-on cap and keeping them in the refrigerator.

To Store Lemon and Orange Zest

If you have grated too much orange or lemon zest or if you simply must prepare it in advance, you can store it for several days. Just put the zest in a small sealed container, containing as little air as possible, and refrigerate.

Braised Lamb Liver

Level of Difficulty	
Preparation Time	15 min
Cost per Serving	$ $
Number of Servings	6
Nutritional Value	278 calories 32.7 g protein 16.9 mg iron
Food Exchanges	4 oz meat 1-1/2 fat exchanges
Cooking Time	9 min
Standing Time	3 min
Power Level	100%, 70%
Write Your Cooking Time Here	

Ingredients
900 g (2 lb) whole lamb livers
45 mL (3 tablespoons) butter
2 onions, finely sliced
1 green pepper, cut into strips
30 mL (2 tablespoons) chili sauce
1 mL (1/4 teaspoon) thyme
75 mL (1/3 cup) coffee

Method
— Preheat a browning dish at 100% for 7 minutes; add the butter and heat at 100% for 30 seconds.
— Sear the liver and then add the onions and green pepper. Set aside.
— Combine the chili sauce, thyme and coffee in a bowl, mix well and pour over the liver and vegetables.
— Cook uncovered for 4 minutes at 70%.
— Turn the dish and continue to cook at 70% for 4 to 5 minutes.
— Let stand for 3 minutes before serving.

This delicious, easy-to-prepare recipe is a real feast for people who like liver. First assemble the required ingredients.

After searing the liver in butter in a preheated browning dish, add the vegetables.

Pour the sauce (made by combining the chili sauce, thyme and coffee) over the liver and vegetables.

Lamb Meatballs

Level of Difficulty	
Preparation Time	15 min
Cost per Serving	$
Number of Servings	4
Nutritional Value	329 calories 24.5 g protein 1.7 mg iron
Food Exchanges	3 oz meat 1/4 vegetable exchange 1 fruit exchange 1/2 fat exchange
Cooking Time	11 min
Standing Time	2 min
Power Level	100%, 90%
Write Your Cooking Time Here	

Ingredients
450 g (1 lb) ground lamb
15 mL (1 tablespoon) soy sauce
1 clove garlic, finely chopped
15 mL (1 tablespoon) beef stock concentrate (Bovril)
15 mL (1 tablespoon) oil
250 mL (1 cup) broccoli flowerets
75 mL (1/3 cup) Chinese-style plum sauce, available at speciality grocery shops

Method
— Combine the ground lamb, soy sauce, garlic and beef stock concentrate.
— Shape into meatballs.
— Heat the oil in a dish for 1 minute at 100%.
— Reduce the power level to 90%, place the meatballs in the hot oil and cook for 4 minutes.
— Stir and add the broccoli.
— Cover and cook for 4 to 5 minutes at 90%.
— Add the plum sauce, mix well, increase the power level to 100% and cook for 1 minute.
— Let stand for 2 minutes before serving.

Assemble all the ingredients required for this Oriental-style recipe.

After combining the ground lamb, soy sauce, garlic and beef stock concentrate, shape the mixture into meatballs.

Add the broccoli flowerets after the meatballs have cooked for 4 minutes.

Ragoût of Lamb

Level of Difficulty	🍴
Preparation Time	10 min
Cost per Serving	$
Number of Servings	10
Nutritional Value	318 calories 36.3 g protein 2.3 mg iron
Food Exchanges	4 oz meat 1 fat exchange
Cooking Time	16 min
Standing Time	3 min
Power Level	100%
Write Your Cooking Time Here	

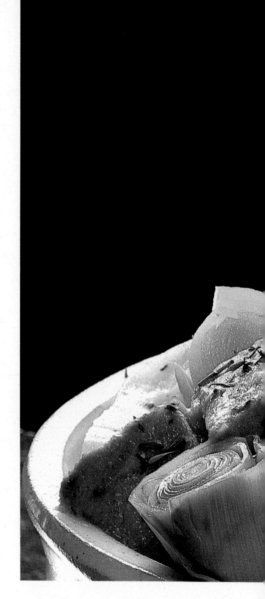

Ingredients
1.3 kg (3 lb) cooked lamb, cut into cubes
45 ml (3 tablespoons) butter
45 ml (3 tablespoons) whole wheat flour
250 ml (1 cup) water
250 ml (1 cup) lamb stock
1 leek, sliced across
salt and pepper to taste

Method
— Melt the butter in a dish for 1 minute at 100%.
— Add the flour, mix well and pour in the water and lamb stock, stirring well.
— Cook for 5 to 6 minutes at 100%, stirring every 2 minutes; set the resulting sauce aside.
— Put the leek in a dish and add 30 ml (2 tablespoons) water; cook for 4 to 5 minutes at 100%.
— Add the leeks and the cooked lamb to the sauce and heat for 3 to 4 minutes at 100%.
— Let stand for 3 minutes before serving.

MICROTIPS

To Prevent Ground Meat from Sticking to Your Fingers

It is really very simple to prevent ground meat from sticking to your fingers when you are preparing meat loaf; simply wet your hands with cold water just before you start to knead the meat.

To Check Whether a Meat Loaf Is Done

If you don't have a meat thermometer, you can still get a good idea of how well done your meat loaf is. Here's how:

1. Pierce the center of the loaf with a skewer and press down on the loaf.

2. Check the juice that seeps out. If it is very clear, the loaf is done. If not, continue to cook for 2 minutes at most and repeat this procedure.

Entertaining

Menu:
Cucumber Salad
Consommé Madrilène
Rolled Breast of Veal
Apricot Flan

Having friends or relatives to dine is something we would all like to be able to do more often. Not only is it enjoyable for the guests who, besides getting together, might make a gastronomic discovery or two but for you as well, who will find the experience both enjoyable and challenging. You are responsible for choosing what dishes to serve as well as for preparing them so as to bring out the best in each. And you also have the task of presenting the dishes so that they are as harmonious with each other in a visual sense as they are in flavor.

We would all agree this constitutes quite a challenge. But your success will be generously recognized and you are bound to find pleasure in having lived up to everyone's expectations.

The menu we are proposing here has all the necessary ingredients for success. Each dish has its own distinctive flavor and, complementing each other nicely, the overall meal will be relaxed and refined.

From the Recipe to Your Table

If you don't want the meal to become a bothersome task, it is important to plan well. A meal cooked in the microwave oven must be planned just like one that is cooked in a conventional oven. Cooking and reheating times are the only things that vary.

The morning before the meal:
— Prepare the apricot flan.
8 hours before the meal:
— Prepare the consommé.
3-1/2 hours before the meal:
— Make the cucumber salad.
1-1/2 hours before the meal:
— Prepare the rolled breast of veal.

Cucumber Salad

Ingredients
2 English cucumbers
10 mL (2 teaspoons) salt
125 mL (1/2 cup) white
vinegar
50 mL (1/4 cup) sugar
30 mL (2 tablespoons) aniseed
1 mL (1/4 teaspoon) white
pepper
30 mL (2 tablespoons) parsley,
chopped

Method
— Cut the cucumbers into
  very thin slices, add the
  salt and mix well.
— Let stand for one hour at
  room temperature.
— Drain the cucumber and
  then add the vinegar,
  sugar, aniseed and
  pepper; mix well.
— Refigerate for 3 hours.
— Sprinkle with parsley
  before serving.

Consommé Madrilène

Ingredients
900 g (2 lb) beef shank
225 g (8 oz) ground beef
1 L (4 cups) water
1 796 mL (28 oz) can
tomatoes, chopped
1 onion, chopped
1 carrot, cut into sticks
1 clove garlic, chopped
pinch thyme
salt and pepper to taste
1 envelope gelatin

Method
— In a casserole, combine all
  the ingredients except the
  gelatin and mix well.
  Cover and cook for 1
  hour at 100%, stirring
  halfway through the
  cooking time.
— Set aside for 1 hour and
  then strain.
— Measure 500 mL (2 cups)
  of the resulting consommé
  and heat for 7 to 9

minutes at 100%.
— Measure 125 mL (1/2 cup)
  of the cooled consommé
  and soak the gelatin in it
  for 1 minute; stir and add
  to the hot consommé.
— Stir the mixture well and
  heat for 2 minutes at
  100%.
— Pour into individual bowls
  and refrigerate for 6 hours
  before serving.

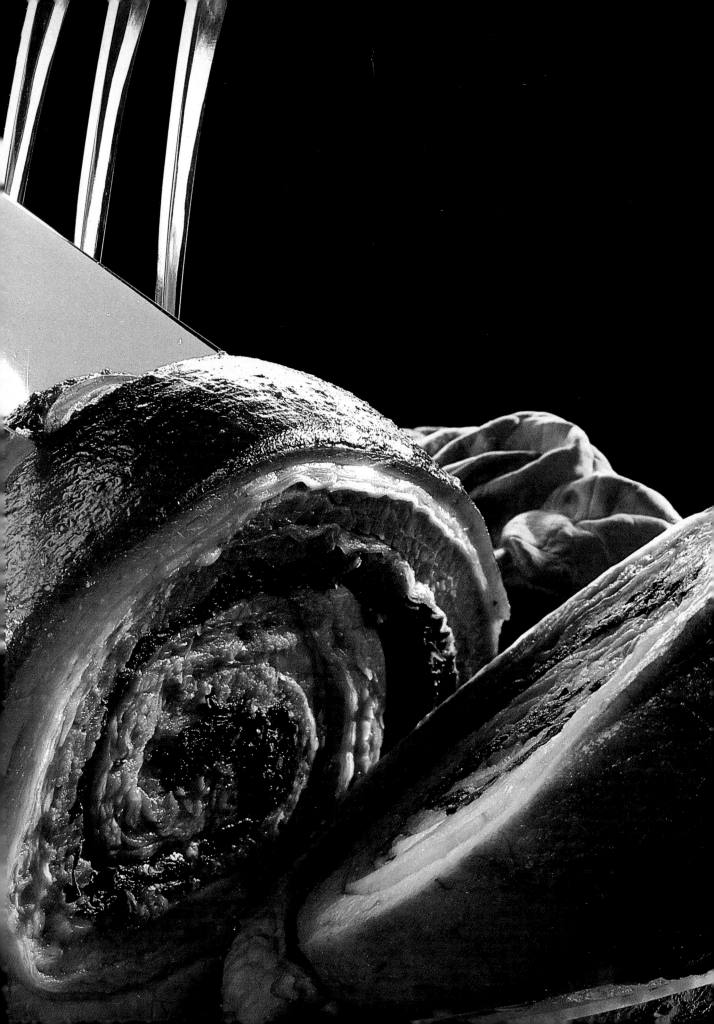

Veal Breast Stuffed with Spinach and Ham

Level of Difficulty	🍴🍴
Preparation Time	20 min
Cost per Serving	$ $ $
Number of Servings	6
Nutritional Value	317 calories 44.4 g protein 5.3 mg iron
Food Exchanges	4 oz meat 1 vegetable exchange 1 fat exchange 1/4 milk exchange
Cooking Time	1 h 15 min
Standing Time	10 min
Power Level	70%, 100%
Write Your Cooking Time Here	

Ingredients
900 (2 lb) veal breast, boned
225 g (8 oz) cooked ham
450 g (1 lb) spinach, cooked and drained
15 mL (1 tablespoon) Dijon mustard
15 mL (1 tablespoon) oil

Sauce:
15 mL (1 tablespoon) butter
15 mL (1 tablespoon) flour
250 mL (1 cup) milk
30 mL (2 tablespoons) Dijon mustard
juice of 1 lemon
salt and pepper to taste
pinch nutmeg
fresh watercress, chopped

Method
— Pound the veal breast gently with the blunt side of a mallet; place the cooked ham and spinach over the veal.
— Roll up and tie with string.
— Combine the mustard and oil, and brush the roll with the mixture.
— Place the roll on a meat rack and cook uncovered for 30 minutes at 70%.
— Give the rack a half-turn and continue to cook at 70% for 30 to 40 minutes, or until the meat is done.
— Remove the roll from the oven and cover it with aluminum foil, putting the shiny side next to the meat.
— Let stand for 10 minutes.
— To make the sauce, melt the butter in a dish for 30 seconds at 100%; add the flour and mix well.
— Pour in the milk and cook at 100% for 3 to 4 minutes or until the mixture thickens, stirring 3 times during the cooking.
— Add the mustard, lemon juice and seasonings; mix well.
— When the roll has stood for the required time, cover with the sauce and sprinkle with watercress. Serve.

Apricot Flan

Ingredients
1 455 mL (16 oz) can apricot halves
250 mL (1 cup) whole wheat flour
175 mL (3/4 cup) walnuts, chopped
90 mL (6 tablespoons) butter
1 mL (1/4 teaspoon) cinnamon
45 mL (3 tablespoons) sugar
pinch salt
8 egg yolks
500 mL (2 cups) milk
50 mL (1/4 cup) cornstarch
75 mL (1/3 cup) sugar
3 mL (3/4 teaspoon) almond extract
50 mL (1/4 cup) apple jelly

Method
— Combine the flour, chopped nuts, butter, cinnamon, 45 mL (3 tablespoons) sugar, salt and 2 egg yolks and beat until the mixture is of an even consistency.
— Line a 25 cm (10 in) quiche dish with the mixture.
— Prick the bottom with a fork in a few places.
— Put the dish on a raised rack in the oven and cook at 70% for 4 to 5 minutes, giving the dish a half-turn once during the cooking time.
— Set aside to cool.
— In a bowl, combine the milk, cornstarch and 75 mL (1/3 cup) sugar.
— Cook at 100% for 4 to 5 minutes, stirring every 2 minutes, and set aside.
— Beat 6 egg yolks while adding a little of the hot milk mixture.
— Gently pour the egg mixture into the hot milk mixture.
— Cook at 100% for 1 to 2 minutes, stirring once during the cooking time. Do not allow to boil.
— Add the almond extract and mix.
— Cover with plastic wrap, placing it directly against the surface of the mixture, and refrigerate for 30 minutes.
— Pour the mixture into the cooled crust and refrigerate for about 4 hours.
— Place the apricots on top.
— Melt the apple jelly for 1 minute at 50% and brush over the apricots to give a glazed effect.

MICROTIPS

To Marinate Veal or Lamb Effectively

Many veal and lamb lovers find chops, ribs and cubes that have been marinated before braising truly delicious. To obtain as much flavor as possible from a marinade, follow these four rules:

1. Use fresh meat rather than meat that has been frozen.

2. Marinate the meat right after you buy it. Not only will fresh meat take up the flavor of the marinade better but it will retain the flavor longer.

3. Using a fork, prick the entire surface and the sides of the meat. This will enable the meat to absorb more of the marinade, giving it more flavor.

4. Stir the marinade from time to time and move the pieces of meat around in it.

Veal and Lamb Terminology

Baby (milk-fed) lamb: Very young lamb that is called "white lamb" *(agneau blanc),* as opposed to grey, or "grass-fed" lamb (see below). Slaughtered before it has been weaned, this lamb has a rich milk-based diet and its meat is extremely tender when cooked.

Baby (milk-fed) veal: Very young calf, generally slaughtered before the age of eight weeks, that is, before it has been weaned. Also known as provimi veal, its meat is very tender, very pale pink, and has no marbling. It has less flavor and nutritional value than veal as we know it. It is quite rare and therefore very expensive.

Bard: To arrange and tie strips of bacon or pork fat on the surface of a piece of lean meat to give it additional flavor and moisture during the cooking.

Baron of lamb: A large cut made up of the English saddle and the two legs. The term can also be used for a smaller cut, one that includes the saddle of the leg rather than the whole saddle.

Blanquette: A white stew traditionally made with veal as its base. The meat is never seared before stewing. The sauce is thickened with cream and egg yolks and flavored with lemon juice. The classic version always contains pearl onions and button mushrooms.

Escallops: A very thin, lean slice of veal which is normally taken from the round (upper and lower leg). It is frequently served breaded, with or without a sauce.

Grass-fed lamb: Lamb intended for butchering that has grazed in the pasture. Its fat has therefore lost its whiteness—which is why it is sometimes called gray lamb *(agneau gris).* Grey lamb should be distinguished from the "white lamb" *(agneau blanc)* or "milk-fed lamb" (see *Baby (milk-fed) lamb*).

Lard:	To make slits in a cut of lean meat and insert small strips of pork fat, or ''lardons.'' This technique prevents lean meat from drying out during slow cooking.
Marbling:	The small rivulets of fat found through most types of meat. The meat of young calves and lambs has hardly any marbling, while that of older animals, if of high quality, has light to moderate marbling.
Medallions of veal:	Special cuts of veal taken from the loin. These small circular pieces are extremely tender and usually served with a sauce.
Mutton:	Some breeding schools consider that lamb becomes mutton when the animal is more than one year old while others make a more detailed assessment before including it in this category. The taste of young mutton is stronger, of course, than that of lamb, and it is best to trim the fat off before cooking. The meat is still tender, however.
Paupiette:	A thin slice of meat covered with stuffing and rolled, sometimes barded, and then braised or steamed in parchment paper. Paupiettes made of veal are among the favorites.
Sauté of lamb or veal:	Cubes of equal size taken from the shoulder which are first sautéed and then braised in a thickened liquid.
Sweetbread:	A variety meat of calf and lamb, white in color. Sweetbread is the name given in cookery to the thymus gland, situated in the upper part of the chest. Only the round part is edible. Calf and lamb sweetbreads are prepared in more or less the same way, but the former is more prized. Sweetbreads are also used in garnishes, stuffing and stews.

Conversion Chart

Conversion Chart for the Main Measures Used in Cooking

Volume		Weight	
1 teaspoon	5 mL	2.2 lb	1 kg (1000 g)
1 tablespoon	15 mL	1.1 lb	500 g
		0.5 lb	225 g
1 quart (4 cups)	1 litre	0.25 lb	115 g
1 pint (2 cups)	500 mL		
1/2 cup	125 mL		
1/4 cup	50 mL	1 oz	30 g

Metric Equivalents for Cooking Temperatures

°C	°F	°C	°F
49°C	120°F	120°C	250°F
54°C	130°F	135°C	275°F
60°C	140°F	150°C	300°F
66°C	150°F	160°C	325°F
71°C	160°F	180°C	350°F
77°C	170°F	190°C	375°F
82°C	180°F	200°C	400°F
93°C	200°F	220°C	425°F
107°C	225°F	230°C	450°F

Readers will note that, in the recipes, we give 250 mL as the equivalent for 1 cup and 450 g as the equivalent for 1 lb and that fractions of these measurements are even less mathematically accurate. The reason for this is that mathematically accurate conversions are just not practical in cooking. Your kitchen scales are simply not accurate enough to weigh 454 g—the true equivalent of 1 lb—and it would be a waste of time to try. The conversions given in this series, therefore, necessarily represent approximate equivalents, but they will still give excellent results in the kitchen. No problems should be encountered if you adhere to either metric or imperial measurements throughout a recipe.

Index

MICROTIPS